S0-APP-256

PETER HAINING is a writer
and anthologizer with a special interest
in the macabre and the occult,
particularly witchcraft and black magic.
His books have been published
in England, in America, and
throughout Europe.

Prentice-Hall, Inc., Englewood Cliffs, New Jersey 07632

Library of Congress Cataloging in Publication Data

Haining, Peter.
A dictionary of ghost lore.

Reprint. Originally published: A dictionary of ghosts.
London : R. Hale, 1982.
1. Ghosts—Dictionaries. I. Title.
BF1444.H34 1984 133.1'0321 83-27083
ISBN 0-13-210485-7
ISBN 0-13-210477-6 (A Reward book : pbk.)

© 1984 by Peter Haining; Robert Hale, Ltd.; and Prentice-Hall, Inc., Englewood Cliffs, New Jersey 07632. All rights reserved. No part of this book may be reproduced in any form or by any means without permission in writing from the publisher. Printed in the United States of America.

10 9 8 7 6 5 4 3 2 1

1. scannable ISBN

2. scannable ISBN (pbk.)

Previously published as *A Dictionary of Ghosts*
by Robert Hale, Ltd., London, 1982. © Peter Haining 1982.

Editorial/production supervision: Marlys Lehmann
Cover design: Neil Stuart
Manufacturing buyer: Doreen Cavallo

This book is available at a special discount when ordered in bulk quantities. Contact Prentice-Hall, Inc., General Publishing Division, Special Sales, Englewood Cliffs, N.J. 07632.

Prentice-Hall International, Inc., *London*
Prentice-Hall of Australia Pty. Limited, *Sydney*
Prentice-Hall Canada Inc., *Toronto*
Prentice-Hall of India Private Limited, *New Delhi*
Prentice-Hall of Japan, Inc., *Tokyo*
Prentice-Hall of Southeast Asia Pte. Ltd., *Singapore*
Whitehall Books Limited, *Wellington, New Zealand*
Editora Prentice-Hall do Brasil Ltda., *Rio de Janeiro*

For
PHILIPPA
with love

Illustrations

Preface

"Then a spirit passed before my face; the hair of my flesh stood up."
The Book of Job

According to a recent survey, 44 percent of the people canvassed believed in the existence of ghosts, and of these one in seven claimed that they had seen, heard, or been haunted by a ghost. The poll also revealed that over half the nation believed in some kind of psychic phenomena.[1] Another similar wide-ranging survey found that the belief there in ghosts was even stronger: over 57 percent of the adult population believed in their existence.[2]

Such facts, even though they are, of course, based on only a representative sample of men and women from all walks of life, still point to a remarkable belief in a subject that has always been surrounded by controversy. Indeed, few would deny it is a subject as fascinating as it is debatable—considered by some to be worthy of the most intensive investigation, but by others as little more than a fantasy developed by over-imaginative minds.

The idea of ghosts—disembodied figures believed to be the spirits of people who have died—has been a part of the human tradition from the very earliest times, and the mixture of belief and disbelief that we share today is very little different from that of our forebears. While the march of knowledge, science, and technology has done much to change mankind's old conceptions, it has done little either to change our opinions about ghosts or explain the reason for them. No doubt this element of mystery is one of the important reasons for our interest's remaining so strong through the passing years.

The topic has, naturally enough, given rise to a veritable library of books on ghosts and hauntings, many based on personal experience, others on painstaking research. They range from the superb to the tawdry, from the objective to the sensational. To read them all in the search for answers to this mystery would certainly take a lifetime. So why, the reader may ask, has yet another volume been added to this enormous collection? Simply, because no one has attempted a dictionary of this kind before. No other writer, to my knowledge, has tried to define the various types of ghosts found around the world, catalogued the famous historical hauntings, and detailed the authorities and personalities associated with the subject over the years. Not in a single volume, at any rate!

This dictionary does not claim to be exhaustive—the subject is so vast that it would not be possible to embrace every element in anything less than several volumes. But it *is* representative and does, I believe, give a very fair coverage of the topic in a way which should prove useful to both the expert and the layman. It is based on twenty-five years of involvement with

[1] *News of the World*, January 4, 1981.

[2] *Daily Mail*, October 21, 1979.

the subject as both researcher and investigator. Many of the entries are substantiated by the words of much greater experts than I, and where such authorities are not given, the opinions are my own based on a multiplicity of sources. In a sentence, if some aspect of the lore of ghosts and hauntings interests you, I hope you will find both the requisite entry and basic information you require herein. In most instances the signposts to further reading on the topic are also given.

As to my own belief in ghosts I find the evidence that such beings—entities spirits—call them what you will—exist to be most convincing. I, personally, have met too many genuine people convinced of their own experiences, as well as having read more than enough authentic accounts, to deny such a possibility. I hope, therefore, if you should dip into this work as a complete skeptic, you might find enough evidence in both words and pictures to rethink your views. Certainly those large percentages of people in both America and Britain—not to mention the other nations for whom I do not have current figures, but who are well represented in the entries that follow—are more than a little convinced there is.

All Houses in which men have lived and died
Are Haunted houses: through the open doors
The harmless phantoms on their errands glide
With Feet that make no sound upon the floors.

Henry Wordsworth Longfellow
(1807–82)

ACTORS

Members of the acting profession are widely considered to be the group of people with the strongest belief in, and most healthy respect for, ghosts and superstitions. Indeed, their fraternity is riddled with quaint superstitions that must be observed to ensure success when appearing on stage—to ignore these omens is said to court disaster. Many of these superstitions have been discussed in a number of books, including Philippa Waring's comprehensive *Dictionary of Omens and Superstitions* (1978). In this she mentions that most actors are firm believers in ghosts and that not a few famous theaters are reputed to be haunted. Members of the profession also have a delightful phrase that is often used: "My ghost walked on Friday." This is not meant literally, of course, but is actually theatrical slang to indicate they have been paid their wages! Perhaps not surprisingly, a number of theatrical ghosts are said to be those of people who were once actors themselves. For instance, one of Britain's most famous comedians, Dan Leno, haunts the Theatre Royal in London's Drury Lane, and the comic Stanley Lupino says that while appearing in a pantomime there he both saw and spoke to Leno. The Theatre Royal is also said to be haunted by the ghost of the great dramatic actor Charles Kean, as well as a man in gray believed to be the spirit of an unfortunate soul bricked up alive in the walls of the building many years ago. The Adelphi Theatre in London is haunted by the handsome Victorian matinee idol, William Terris, who was stabbed to death at the stage door in 1897. Perhaps, though, the most famous ghost story of all is that told by Sir Alec Guinness, who says that while he was playing *Hamlet* at the Old Vic he was suddenly startled to see the figure of William Shakespeare looking up at him from the stalls! Shakespeare, it should be added, figures prominently in several theatrical superstitions, and his play *Macbeth* is believed to be unlucky to appear in; no actor of experience will ever quote from it—in particular from the famous "witches' scene," which is thought to have the power to raise evil spirits and doom the production.

ADVERTISEMENT

Perhaps the strangest advertisement ever recorded in the annals of the supernatural was this one, which appeared in the London *Morning Post* of February 27, 1919.

> *Haunted or Disturbed Properties*. A lady who has deeply studied this subject and possesses unusual powers, will find out the history of the trouble and undertake to remedy it. Houses with persistent bad luck can often be freed from the influence. Strictest confidence. Social references asked and offered.

A photographic interpretation of the ghostly actor-manager who haunts the Theatre Royal, London

AFRIT

The Arabian afrit is the spirit of a man who has been murdered and rises to avenge the murder. According to an ancient tradition, the afrit emerges from the slain person's blood wherever it falls on the ground, materializing rather like smoke from a fire. The activities of these spirits can be quite terrifying, and the only way to prevent their appearing is to drive a new nail into the ground where the murder was committed. Experts have noted that this tradition—known as "nailing down the ghost"—has a certain similarity with the method prescribed in European folklore for dealing with vampires.

AIRCRAFT GHOSTS

Ghosts have been reported on a number of aircraft during recent years and in October 1974, the London *Evening News* carried a story that cleaners at Heathrow Airport had claimed there was a sinister force at work on certain of the planes. An airport official was quoted as saying, "We have had reports about some strange presence on the jumbo jet planes and at present it cannot be explained. Some cleaners have said they have been thrown about by something invisible and others that they have been unable to move, as if they were being held down by something." The most famous story of an airline haunting is that told by the American investigative writer, John G. Fuller, in his book *The Ghost of Flight 401* (1978) about the phantoms that haunt a number of planes belonging to Eastern Airlines. In 1973 an L-1011 TriStar belonging to Eastern Airlines—Flight 401—crashed near Florida killing nearly 100 people, among whom were the pilot, Captain Bob Loft, and the engineer, Don Repo. Not long thereafter, other crews flying Eastern Airlines' TriStars began to report seeing ghostly figures that looked remarkably like Loft and Repo on board their aircraft. In every case the figures seemed friendly and appeared to want only to prevent any other TriStar from suffering the same tragedy as had befallen them. Subsequently John Fuller investigated the story and published his book, and although considerable mystery still hangs over the haunting it remains the best-known story of ghosts that took to the skies. As Fuller himself remarked, "If you believe that old country mansions are haunted, why not a jumbo jet?"

AMHERST MYSTERY

The Amherst Mystery is perhaps the most famous case of a poltergeist on the North American continent. It took place during the years 1878 and 1879 in the small township of Amherst in Nova Scotia and concerned the strange occurrences that went on there in a small timber-frame house. The mysterious noises, movement of objects, and messages scratched onto the walls were centered on a nineteen-year-old girl, Esther Cox, and followed shortly after her ill-fated courtship by a man named Bob McNeal who attempted to rape her in August 1878. In the months that followed, Esther was subjected to numerous attacks by the poltergeist, which also left several dramatic messages scrawled on the walls of the house, including one in foot-high letters that read, "Esther Cox you are mine to kill." What has made this affair so remarkable is that the phenomena were actually seen occurring by a number of highly respectable witnesses, including two local clergymen and a neighbor, Walter Hubbell, who, though initially skeptical, eventually became so convinced the poltergeist was genuine that he wrote what is now considered the classic study of the events, *The Great Amherst Mystery* (1879). When the controversy was at its height, the ghost ceased its attacks as suddenly and mysteriously as they had begun. Esther Cox herself soon left Nova Scotia and settled in America, where she refused to speak again about the terrifying events that had surrounded her, for fear, as she said, that they "might begin again."

AMITYVILLE HORROR

The Amityville Horror is the most notorious alleged haunting to have been reported recently. A book of the same title written in 1978 by Jay Anson (Prentice-Hall) became a multimillion dollar bestseller around the world. The film made a year later was an equal sensation. The haunting took place in a typical suburban American home in the town of Amityville on Long Island, New York, in December 1975, immediately after George and Kathy Lutz moved in with their three children. In the next twenty-eight days they were assailed by all manner of ghostly phenomena and finally fled the house in terror. The reason for these poltergeist-like happenings was said to be the fact that a previous resident, twenty-four-year-old Ronald De Feo, had murdered his sleeping parents and two brothers and sisters in the house. Despite the impressive documentation of Anson's book, *The Amityville Horror*, many doubts have been recently expressed by experts in the supernatural about the authenticity of the story.

ANGAKOK

The angakok is an Eskimo medium, or shaman, who has the power to communicate with spirits and raise the ghosts of the dead. The Eskimos believe any misfortune at sea is caused by the ghosts of their ancestors and consequently make frequent offerings to them.

ANGELS OF MONS

The First World War ghost story of the Angels of Mons is one of the most curious in the annals of the supernatural: curious because though the man who first wrote about the legend insisted it was a work of fiction, many reports were later received from soldiers who claimed they had actually *seen* the phantom bowmen! The story began on September 29, 1914—St Michael's Day—when the Welsh author and journalist Arthur Machen (1863–1947) published a story called "The Bowmen" in the London *Evening News*. The inspiration for his story had been the terrible Battle of Mons on August 23, 1914, when British troops, outnumbered by ten to one, had held fifty German divisions at bay and helped enormously in the French withdrawal. So moved was he by this bravery, that Machen wrote a short story about a British soldier, who, staring defeat in the face, had uttered a Latin prayer and then seen a group of phantom bowmen firing their flights of silvery arrows into the advancing German forces. The amazed soldier and his colleagues saw the

The famous First World War incident of the Angels of Mons as depicted by A. Forestier

enemy troops fall by the hundreds and when later they examined the bodies, found they bore not a single wound. In the depressed climate of Britain that autumn of 1914, the inspiring story of "The Bowmen" was enthusiastically received by countless readers. But a curious sequel then occurred. Slowly, reports began to filter back from France that troops there had actually *seen* the ghostly saviors in the sky; they were not bowmen, however, but angels. Although there were some variations in these accounts, the basic facts were the same. Dozens of soldiers claimed they had witnessed the appearance of phantom figures in the sky who rained death on the advancing enemy. As soon as he began to hear these accounts, Arthur Machen quickly protested that he had made up the story—that there was no truth in it. But few people would listen. The account was so inspirational they *wanted* to believe God was on the Allies' side. So the legend of the Angels of Mons was born. It remains famous to this day, and the part played in it by Machen and the soliders who deepened the mystery are studied in Ralph Shirley's *The Angel Warriors at Mons* (1918).

ANIMAL GHOSTS

Various experts on the supernatural are agreed that animal ghosts do exist and function in much the same way as the spirits of human beings. As Christina Hole has written so touchingly in her *Haunted England* (1940), "No one who has ever loved a horse, a dog or a cat can possibly believe that faithful friend to be a mere soulless creature that lives for a few years and then dies forever." And ghost-hunter Elliott O'Donnell has even devoted a whole book to the topic, *Animal Ghosts* (1913), in which he says emphatically, "The mere fact that there are manifestations of 'dead' people proves some kind of life after death for human beings; and happily the same proof is available with regard to a future life for animals; indeed there are as many animal phantasms as human—perhaps more." Under the various headings throughout this book, the reader will find specific references to animal ghosts such as cats, dogs, horses, birds. Another recent survey of note is *Animal Ghosts* by Raymond Bayless (1970).

ANKOU

The ankou or graveyard watcher is the ghost who guards cemeteries and stories of him are found throughout Europe. Whenever a new graveyard was created, it was customary to bury some unfortunate victim alive in the first grave so that a ghostly guardian was created. This ankou would then frighten off anyone—living or dead—who might come to disturb the peace of the departed. The graveyard watcher is said to be the cause of that involuntary shiver that often causes a person to remark that "someone is walking over my grave!"

APPARITION

An apparition is a figure which gives all the appearance of being someone the viewer knows to be either a long way off at that moment, or else dead. The tradition of apparitions goes back to the earliest times and historical records are full of accounts of people seeing such figures which evidence suggests were neither caused by illusion nor deception of the senses. These stories indicate that apparitions are not always seen, but can also be either felt or heard. The three main kinds of apparitions are: crisis apparitions, where illness, danger or death is involved; haunting apparitions, where a single figure is seen repeatedly in the same place; and experimental apparitions, where a person still alive projects an appearance of himself before the view of another. Recently, considerable research has been done into this topic by the

The grim ankou or graveyard watcher, from a nineteenth-century engraving

Institute of Psychophysical Research in Great Britain, which based its findings on some 1,800 cases. A major discovery was that far from all the apparitions being of dead people, about a third of those reported were of people still alive. As to whether perceivers realized that they were seeing an apparition—the report said that 46 per cent were aware of the fact at once, 18 per cent not immediately, 5 per cent as the experience ended and 31 per cent not until after it had ended. The survey also found that on the whole apparitions that occlude light (for instance when looking in at a window) are rare, but not unknown. A considerable variation was noted in the feelings of those who had seen apparitions: some were very frightened, some not in the least frightened and some only experienced fear and disturbance later. Instances were also discovered when people were actually stimulated by what they had seen. This fascinating survey is discussed in detail by two of the institute's researchers, Celia Green and Charles McCreery, in their book, *Apparitions* (1975). Two other earlier and equally important studies are *Apparitions and Haunted Houses* by Sir Ernest Bennett (1939) and *Apparitions* by G. N. M. Tyrrell (1953).

ARMISTICE DAY FRAUD

On November 11, 1922, Armistice Day, which celebrated the end of the First World War, Mrs. Ada Emma Deane, an English charwoman whose hobby was photography, claimed to have taken a photograph at the Cenotaph in London on which appeared the faces of a number of dead soldiers. The picture immediately created a sensation, and Mrs. Deane became famous overnight. On the following November 11 and again on the same day in 1924 she produced further photographs of the faces of soldiers. In the meantime she also set herself up as a spirit photographer, seemingly able to take pictures of anyone who had died—at a price, of course. Then just after Armistice Day in 1924, a photographic agency in London spotted something rather strange about the faces at the Cenotaph; they were all identical to those of sportsmen that the agency had recently photographed for the national newspapers! This revelation brought a sudden end to Mrs. Deane's activities and she hastily disappeared from public view.

ART

Ghosts have featured in the work of great artists and painters for centuries, and some of the best examples of their skill are to be found on the walls of famous museums around the world—pictures like William Hogarth's *Lovat's Ghost on Pilgrimage, Speak—Speak!* by Sir John Millais, and Frederick Remington's beautiful *Ghost of the Indian Maiden*. As an anonymous contributor to the *Strand Magazine* of December 1904 writing on "Ghosts in Art" has observed, "Ghosts of mortals—especially of beautiful maidens—revisiting their ancient haunts are familiar enough in the countless legends of Europe, and many of these legends have been seized on by the painter." But, he adds, "whatever these ghosts are that 'freeze the blood' and make the hair to 'stand on end like the quills upon the fretful porcupine' it is doubtful whether any artist has succeeded in reproducing the effect." The one artist to disprove this statement is probably George Cruikshank (1792–1878), the caricaturist and illustrator who helped immortalize many of Charles Dickens's finest novels through his evocative pictures. Cruikshank was fascinated by the supernatural and contributed a fine article about ghosts and phantoms entitled "Frights" to Dickens's magazine *All The Year Round* in October 1841. He illustrated it with the grim but somehow delightful engraving reproduced on page 10.

AN ACCOUNT

OF THE

DREADFUL APPARITION

That appeared last night to Henry —— in this street, of Mary ——, the shopkeeper's daughter round the corner, in a shroud, all covered in white.

The castle clock struck one—the night was dark, drear, and tempestuous. —Henry set in an antique chamber of it, over a wood fire, which, in the stupor of contemplation, he had suffered to decrease into a few lifeless embers; on the table by him lay the portrait of Mary—the features of which were not very perfectly disclosed by a taper, that just glimmered in the socket. He took up the portrait, however, and gazing intensely upon it, till the taper, suddenly burning brighter, discovered to him a phenomenon he was not less terrified than surprised at.—The eyes of the portrait moved;—the features from an angelic smile, changed to a look of solemn sadness; a tear stole down each cheek, and the bosom palpitated as with sighing.

Again the clock struck *one*—it had struck the same hour but ten minutes before.—Henry heard the castle gate grate on its hinges—it slammed too—the clock struck one again—and a deadly groan echoed through the castle. Henry was not subject to superstituous fears—neither was he a coward;—yet a hero of romance might have been justified in a case like this, should he have betrayed fear.—Henry's heart sunk within him—his knees smote together, and upon the chamber door being opened, and his name uttered in a hollow voice, he dropped the portrait to the floor; and sat, as if rivitted to the chair, without daring to lift up his eyes. At length, however, as silence again prevailed, he ventured for a moment to raise his eyes, when—my blood freezes as I relate it—before him stood the figure of Mary in a shroud—her beamless eyes fixed upon him with a vacant stare; and her bared bosom exposing a most deadly gash. "Henry, Henry, Henry!" she repeated in a hollow tone—"Henry! I am come for thee! thou hast often said that death with me was preferable to life without me; come then, and enjoy with me all the ecstacies of love these ghastly features, added to the contemplation of a charnel-house, can inspire;" then, grasping his hand with her icy fingers, he swooned; and instantly found himself —— stretched on the hearth of his master's kitchen; a romance in his hand, and the house dog by his side, whose cold nose touching his hand, had awaked him.

Pitts, Printer and Toy Warehouse, Great St. Andrew Street, 7 Dials.

A penny broadsheet—typical of many sold in the eighteenth century

ATHENODORUS

One of the earliest ghost stories on record concerns the Greek philosopher Athenodorus, who lived during the second century A.D. The story is related by Pliny the Younger who says that the philosopher once stayed at a house that was believed to be haunted by a ghost swathed in chains. When the figure appeared to Athenodorus one evening, he followed it out into the garden where it suddenly disappeared over a patch of barren earth. The next day the old Greek had the spot dug up and there found a human skeleton bound in chains. Once these bones had been given a proper burial, says Pliny, the ghost never troubled the house again.

A sleeper awakened by a ghostly visitor—Sir John Millais's famous painting entitled *Speak—Speak!*

"Frights," one of George Cruikshank's marvelous ghostly engravings

John Aubrey—one of the earliest ghost-story collectors

AUBREY, JOHN (1626–97)

Aubrey, the famous antiquary and folklorist, is credited with being one of the first collectors of ghost stories, and his great compilation, *Miscellanies* (1696) is full of tales of phantoms that he had noted down from first-hand accounts gathered all over the country. Aubrey's belief in the supernatural was all the stronger because of a personal experience of hearing some phantom knocking noises in his own home. In his *Miscellanies* he refers to these instances when strange, inexplicable sounds were heard just prior to his father's death. "Three or four days before my father died," he says, "as I was in my bed about nine o'clock in the morning, perfectly awake, I did hear three distinct knocks on the bed's-head, as if it had been with a ruler or ferula." This strange event, and the other testimonies that he gathered, left him totally convinced of the actuality of the spirit world.

B

BAKA

Baka is a Haitian word to describe a ghostly creature not unlike a ghoul that returns after death to eat human flesh. During their natural lives, bakas are said to be members of a secret society which initiates them into the ways they must follow after death.

BANSHEE

The banshee, or bean si as the spirit is correctly described, is "the lady of death" who haunts very ancient Irish families and is unquestionably that country's best-known ghost. She appears just prior to a person's death and announces the fact by wailing and crying. The banshee usually appears within the vicinity of the ancestral home during the night hours and, although the voice is clearly that of a human female, her lamentations are in a language that no one can understand. She may well come to the house several nights running before anyone dies and it is possible that the death forecast

A typical picture of a banshee—Ireland's famous wailing spirit that haunts the country's old families

may be for someone who is staying elsewhere, even abroad. There are on record a number of instances of members of old Irish families dying literally thousands of miles away—as far as Canada and Australia—just as a banshee is wailing outside their birthplace back in Ireland. The banshee materializes either as a beautiful young woman dressed in elegant garments such as a gray cloak over a green dress in the style of the Middle Ages, or as a very old woman, bent and decrepit, enveloped in a winding-sheet or grave dress. Both types of banshee have long hair that streams in the wind and their eyes are fiery red from continual weeping. According to tradition the creature is very shy, easily irritated, and if annoyed will fly away and not return during the same generation. It is also believed that each banshee is the spirit of a much earlier member of the same family who has been appointed as the messenger of death. Families of both high and low estate throughout Ireland are said to have their own banshees. The Scots also have their own form of banshee, the bean-nighe or "little washer by the ford" who appears washing the grave clothes of those about to die. The bean-nighe is the ghost of a woman who died in childbirth, and according to some reports is rather ugly—with only one nostril, large protruding front teeth and long, hanging breasts. Both Scots and Irish banshees are discussed in detail in Elliott O'Donnell's *The Banshee* (1907), which also looks at their history and some strange instances of their appearances in different parts of the world.

BEALING BELLS

For two months in 1834, nine bells in the kitchen of Bealings House in Suffolk, England, were rung almost daily by what could only be described as ghostly hands. Despite the most intensive observation of all the members of the household, the bells continued to ring for no apparent reason and resulted in the story being recorded as a classic poltergeist case. Although there have been numerous other accounts of phantom bell-ringing—several mentioned by Harry Price in his *Poltergeist Over England* (1945) which also deals with the Bealing Bells at some length—this instance has proved quite baffling, all the more so in the light of a detailed and painstaking account of the happenings by the owner of the house, Major Edward Moor, *Bealing Bells: An Account of the Mysterious Ringing of Bells at Great Bealings, Suffolk, in 1834*, which he published in 1841.

BELL WITCH

The Bell Witch was a noisy, troublesome poltergeist that tormented the family of John Bell of Robertson County, Tennessee, from 1817 to 1820, earning a notoriety that spread across the length and breadth of America. The spirit first began to persecute Farmer Bell, his wife and eight children in the late summer of 1817, materializing briefly in the form of strange animals and then making knocking noises inside and outside the home. Later, the ghost took to snatching bedclothes from the sleeping children, and then smacking and pinching those who tried to resist. For a time the Bells kept the story of their ghost a secret, but when news of it leaked out, there followed a constant stream of visitors to the the home—many of whom heard or felt the anger of the phantom which had been named the Bell Witch. After months of hardship, the ghost began to speak to the family and announced the reason for its haunting: "I am nothing more than old Kate Bell's witch, and I'm determined to haunt and torment old Jack Bell as long as he lives." The spirit evidently kept its word, for on December 19, 1820, poor Jack Bell, nearly driven out of his mind, collapsed suddenly and died. Thereafter the ghost was only heard of in suspect circumstances—although to make quite sure it did not terrorize the neighborhood any more, the Bell house was torn down and destroyed. The amazing story is fully documented in *The Bell Witch, A Mysterious Spirit* by a descendant of the family, Charles Bailey Bell (1934).

BENSON, EDWARD FREDERIC (1867–1940)

E. F. Benson is the author of four classic collections of ghost stories, *The Room in the Tower* (1912), *Visible and Invisible* (1923), *Spook Stories* (1928) and *More Spook Stories* (1934), selections from which are almost invariably to be found in any new ghost or horror anthology. One of three writing brothers, E. F. Benson became famous for his novel of high society, *Dodo*, published in 1893, but it was his ghost stories that have kept his name alive to this day. Curiously, none of the Benson brothers married and their previously distinguished line ended when E. F., the last of them to survive, passed on in 1940.

BERGMONCK

Bergmonck is a German word for the terrifying looking figure of a gigantic monk who is said to haunt treasure-bearing mines in that country. According to *A Survey of the Occult* edited by Julian Franklyn (1935), which mentions this ghost, all treasure mines throughout the world are said to be haunted by some kind of demon or guardian spirit.

BERRIMA'S HEADLESS GHOST

Berrima's Headless Ghost has been described as the best-attested ghost story in Australia, and it is also perhaps the weirdest. Berrima is a typical rural Australian town about one hundred miles south of Sydney, and it was here on October 22, 1842, that a woman named Lucretia Dunkley was hanged in the town gaol thereby beginning the now famous haunting. Recounting the story in her book, *Visits from Beyond the Grave* (1975), Joyce Zwarycz says that Lucretia was the licensee of the curiously named local inn, the Three

E. F. Benson, another master of the ghost story

Legs-O'-Man Hotel, and ended her days on the gallows for murdering one of her customers, a wealthy farmer, and stealing 500 sovereigns from his corpse. According to Miss Zwarycz:

> After the hangman had done his work, his victim's head was removed for scientific examination. Thereafter, it is said that Lucretia's headless ghost began to roam the pine trees in front of the gaol. For decades, eyewitnesses, so they say, have recorded seeing the apparition. However, a few years ago the pine trees were cut down and the ghost disappeared. It was thought the wandering spirit had gone for ever, but it was reported to have reappeared as recently as Easter 1961. Two youths camped near the ruins of the "Three Legs-O'-Man" had settled in for the night when they heard sobbing efforts to breathe. On investigation they said they saw the headless spectre of Lucretia moving amid the ruins of her old pub. Alarmed, the two campers packed up with surprising speed and moved on to Canberra.

BIG GREY MAN OF BEN MACDHUI

Ben Macdhui, one of the six main peaks of the Cairngorm Mountains, boasts a famous Scottish ghost known as the Big Grey Man of Ben Macdhui, who has been seen as well as heard for generations. The apparition is said to be about ten feet tall and has long, waving arms. Suggestions have been made that the figure is semi-human in appearance and can make a terrible noise that sounds vaguely like Gaelic speech. A number of recent sightings of the Big Grey Man are given in an interesting report on the phantom in Peter Underwood's *Gazetteer of Scottish and Irish Ghosts* (1973).

BLACK LADY OF DARMSTADT

The Black Lady is a well-known German ghost that haunts the town of Darmstadt, and is said to be the spirit of Marianna, wife of the Grand Duke Ferdinand. Her visits are focused on members of the Hesse Family, and she makes a grim sight being swathed in black funeral garments and a long veil. The Black Lady is an omen of death and a number of her appearances and their sad results are catalogued by Mrs. Hugh Fraser in her book, *A Diplomat's Wife in Many Lands* (1893).

BLACKWOOD, ALGERNON (1869–1951)

Algernon Blackwood is affectionately remembered by many thousands of British radio and television listeners as "the ghost man," having earned this nickname by the effective and chilling way in which for years he recounted stories of the supernatural. As a young man Blackwood traveled extensively and had first-hand encounters with ghosts in both Canada and America—experiences that were to help him bring great authenticity to his uncanny tales. Following the success of his first story, "A Haunted Island" (1899), he poured forth a stream of ingenious and spine-chilling yarns that later appeared in such collections as *The Empty House* (1906), *Day and Night Stories* (1917), *Strange Stories* (1929) and many more. He also created a redoubtable

"The ghost man," Algernon Blackwood, a skillful writer and broadcaster

psychic investigator, John Silence, who was a mirror of himself and his own experiences—a man ever ready to tackle any assignment dealing with the occult or the supernatural. The stories about this character were collected together as *John Silence* (1908).

BLAKE, WILLIAM (1757–1827)

William Blake, the English poet and painter, whose work is now much collected and admired despite public indifference during his lifetime, was sustained throughout his life by a vivid faith in the unseen, being guided and encouraged by continual visitations from the spirit world. A strange man of mystical leanings, Blake said that he was often visited by the ghost of his dead brother, which had first come to him clapping its hands with joy almost immediately after the brother's death. Spirit figures are to be found in many of his paintings as well as vividily described in some of his most beautiful lyrics.

BLUE CAP

The blue cap is a ghostly spirit once said to haunt mines who, if offered gifts, would help miners in their work. He usually appeared in the form of a blue-colored flame and was said to possess enormous strength. If he was not properly treated, however, he would bring disaster to the mine where he dwelt, according to W. Y. E. Wentz in *The Fairy-Faith of Celtic Countries* (1911).

BLUE MAN

The Blue Man is a famous ghost who haunts twelfth-century Arundel Castle in Sussex, England. The ghost is believed to be that of a dashing man-of-fashion, for he is arrayed in a magnificent suit of blue silk, and he is usually to be found moving sedately about the castle library. According to legend this ancestral home of the Dukes of Norfolk has three other ghosts: the spirit of a kitchen boy murdered two hundred years ago; a beautiful young girl all in white who committed suicide by jumping from a tower; and a strange white bird that always appears in the vicinity when a member of the family is about to die.

BOGGART

Boggart is an expression from the north of England to describe a mischievous and often unpleasant type of ghost. They have a habit of crawling into people's bedrooms at night, putting a clammy hand on their faces, and then stripping the bedclothes off them. Lancashire, in particular, abounds with stories of boggarts, according to Elliott O'Donnell in his book, *Dangerous*

Ghosts (1954), who quotes several reports, including two from Blackburn. "A boggart that haunted a farm near Blackburn used to scare the farmer's wife by snatching her baby from under her nose," he writes. "It carried the screaming brat to the kitchen and deposited it none too gently on the hearthstone, to the surprise and indignation of the cook. A cottage not very far from the farm was also haunted by a boggart that frightened the sole occupant, an old woman, by shaking her, pulling her ears, thumping on her chest and gnashing its hideous, long, yellow teeth." According to an old tradition in Lancashire, horseshoes hung on the gate or door of a house will keep boggarts away.

BOGIE

The bogie is a rather unpleasant type of spirit who delights in tormenting and frightening human beings. It was believed these ghosts had the power to steal infants and this gave rise to a warning widely repeated by parents to naughty children: "You had better stop or the bogie-man will get you!" According to folklore, bogies are very dangerous spirits who will attack or at least frighten anyone who does not show them respect. They are said to be black in appearance, rather squat and hairy, and have ugly, grinning faces. It was once thought they were the most powerful among ghosts because they served as the assistants to the Devil during his evil-doing among mankind. They apparently have the ability to change their shapes at will and sometimes make a wailing noise that sounds as if they are calling, "I want my bones." It is believed they can be driven away by holding up an open Bible in front of them. Similar spirits are the bogey-beasts, which take the form of evil-looking creatures about the size of a dog.

BOLEYN, ANNE (*c*. 1504–36)

Anne Boleyn, the second wife of the notorious Henry VIII and mother of the later famous Queen Elizabeth I, has provided one of the most famous ghosts at the Tower of London. After falling from Henry's favor, Anne was imprisoned in the Tower, tried for high treason on trumped-up charges, and then beheaded. Not long afterwards it was said her ghost began to walk in the vicinity of the Tower Chapel, as well as on Tower Hill. For almost four hundred years reports of her gliding figure "strangely illuminated" have been made by guardians of the Tower.

BONNIE PRINCE CHARLIE'S GHOST

As one of Scotland's great heroes, it is not surprising to discover that the ghost of Bonnie Prince Charlie has returned to at least one of his old haunts. According to persistent local reports, the County Hotel in Dumfries is haunted by a male figure dressed in Jacobite costume, and indeed it was here that Prince Charles Edward (as he then was) stayed in 1745. The room he used is now known as Prince Charlie's Room and it is here that his troubled spectre is said to appear.

BOOTH, JOHN WILKES (1838–65)

John Wilkes Booth, the actor who shot President Abraham Lincoln on April 14, 1865, is now condemned to haunt the theater where he committed his terrible act, according to numerous accounts. The assassination took place in Ford's Theatre in Washington and for many years Booth's heavy footfalls have been heard about the building. Because of its sinister reputation, the

John Wilkes Booth, the man who shot Abraham Lincoln and whose ghost afterwards haunted Ford's Theatre, Washington

theater actually stood idle for almost a century until it was restored in 1968. However, both workmen and actors have subsequently reported strange encounters with the phantom, and there is an enduring legend that any actor or actress who attempts to speak lines along the route across the stage where Booth made his escape after the shooting will get them hopelessly confused.

BORGIA FAMILY

Italian tradition says that the Borgias are the country's most haunted family, no doubt stemming from their wicked past. Several descendants have come face to face with the extraordinary and terrifying sight of a ghostly-looking coffin giving off a blue light and on which sits the phantom of one of their forebears! This has invariably proved to be a death omen, the person concerned dying shortly afterwards. Details of this haunting are given in *Secrets of the Past* by Allan Upward (1928).

BORLEY RECTORY

Borley Rectory, a dark and rambling old house that stood in the village of Borley on the border between Essex and Suffolk, was for many years known as "the most haunted in England." However, in recent years serious doubt has been cast on many of the stories told about the haunting, and as the building itself no longer exists, the claim is difficult to substantiate. Much of the fame that Borley Rectory came to enjoy was due to the work of the ghost-hunter Harry Price (1881–1948), whose researches brought to light a supposedly long history of haunting that had all begun in the fourteenth century with the

The ruins of Borley Rectory, for years "the most haunted house in England"

murder of a nun who had had an illicit love affair. Apart from collecting reports of the apparition of this nun being seen in the vicinity, he unearthed tales of a mysterious coach and horses that galloped along the road, visions of a headless man, and all sorts of weird poltergeist-type activities in the house itself—such as objects being thrown about, strange scratching noises and bells ringing inexplicably. When Price actually moved into the rectory with a team of investigators after the previous occupants had fled, there was a noticeable decline in the manifestations, but this did not prevent Price completing his study and publishing his findings in *The Most Haunted House in England* (1940). Although he attributed many of the strange happenings to one of the former residents, Price believed there was genuine evidence of a haunting. The mystery deepened still further when a fire accidentally broke out and gutted the rectory. Even stranger events then occurred—weird apparitions were reported in the ruins and human remains were found in the cellar. Price published a second book, *The End of Borley Rectory* in 1946, which brought the story up to date and in so doing started the controversy that has raged to this day. Perhaps the best-known work denouncing Price and the story of "the most haunted house in England" is *The Haunting of Borley Rectory* by E. J. Dingwall, K. M. Goldney and Trevor Hall (1956), but even this has its glaring faults, and though the rectory itself may no longer stand, its fame and controversy as to what really went on there still persist.

BRAHMADAITYA

The brahmadaitya is the chief among the benign ghosts of India, and is said to be the spirit of a brahmin who has died unmarried. He is apparently very particular about his food, lives in a tree, and is kindly disposed to human beings as long as they do not trespass on his domain. Should they do so, he literally breaks their necks!

BRUTUS'S TWO PHANTOMS

The notorious Marcus Brutus (85–42 B.C.), who played a leading part in the conspiracy against Caesar was, according to Roman legend, haunted by two different phantoms during his lifetime! The first was that of Caesar himself, who appeared to him one night not long after the assassination. The second was a messenger of death who visited him just before his battle with Antony and Octavian at Philippi. According to the story, Brutus was about to go to bed when he suddenly heard a noise and turned to find himself confronted by a ghost "that was horrifying in its gigantic proportions and its pale, emaciated face." The nervous Brutus finally plucked up courage to challenge the phantom as to what it wanted, and the ghost replied, "I am your evil spirit and you will see me again near Philippi." And sure enough during the

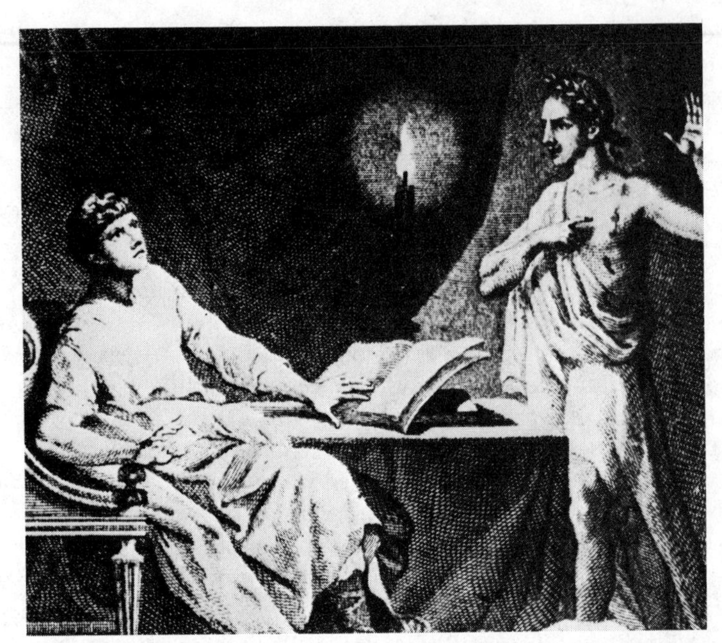

One of the two phantoms that haunted the infamous Marcus Brutus, Caesar's assassin

ill-fated battle that followed, Brutus did see the phantom again just before his death.

BUGABOOS

Despite their ominous name, these Indian ghosts are said to be friendly towards mankind. According to Julian Franklyn in *A Survey of the Occult* (1935) the Indians do not actually believe in the objective existence of these spirits but "mothers use them to quieten naughty children"! The Indians also have two spirits known as Jak and Jakni, male and female entities, whose job it is to guard native villages against other ill-disposed ghosts. However, they are apparently inclined to remove things that appeal to them as presents for each other!

BUGUET, EDOUARD (1841–1901)

Edouard Buguet was a French pioneer of spirit photography whose photographs in the 1860s and 1870s made him world-famous, but which were exposed in 1876 as fraudulent. Unlike his contemporaries in the field, Buguet's pictures were startlingly clear and unmisted, and he went to considerable trouble in imposing the ghostly images on the photographs. Initially he used live models, but when he became afraid his models might be recognized, he switched to employing dummies and sculptured heads. His studio was finally raided by the police after a complaint from a dissatisfied customer, and all the tricks of his trade were discovered. Although Buguet confessed his fraud, he was tried and sentenced to a year's imprisonment. After his release he never again worked as a photographer, but his photographs became much collected and there were still some disciples who believed he had actually photographed spirits of the dead.

BYRON, LORD GEORGE GORDON (1788–1824)

Byron, the gloomy, romantic poet who wrote some of the finest verse in the English language, was deeply interested in the supernatural, and claimed to have seen a phantom monk who haunted Newstead Abbey, the Byron family home. The origin of this ghost was uncertain, one suggestion being that it was a monk who had perished at the hands of an earlier member of the family—but to Byron it was always "the goblin friar." It was said to appear just before any calamity happened to the family, and Byron himself claimed to have seen it shortly before his ill-fated marriage to the heiress Anne Milbanke in 1815. He described it thus:

> *A monk arrayed*
> *In cowl, and beads, and dusky garb appeared,*
> *Now in the moonlight, and now lapsed in shade,*
> *With steps that trod as heavy, yet unheard.*

Lord Byron, the famous poet, who saw a ghost called "the goblin friar," which haunted his family

C

"CANTERVILLE GHOST, THE"

"The Canterville Ghost" is still regarded as one of the most famous and funny ghost stories, despite being almost one hundred years old. It was written in 1887 by the flamboyant and ultimately doomed genius, Oscar Wilde (1854–1900) and is now as highly regarded by lovers of supernatural fiction as Wilde's grim masterpiece, *The Picture of Dorian Gray* (1891).

CAPE TOWN CASTLE GHOST

Cape Town Castle, built in 1665, is the oldest building in South Africa, and also houses the country's oldest ghost. For almost three hundred years a tall, luminous figure has walked along the battlements, disappearing over the edge at the approach of any human being. As recently as 1947, the apparition was seen by two soldiers of the Union Defense Force, but when they tried to get closer, "we were staggered to see it step out over one of the ramparts and vanish into space." The two men looked down about fifty feet into what used to be the moat, but there was no sign of anything. This and another report of a second ghost in the castle called "the Lady in the Gray Hood" are discussed in Eric Rosenthal's *They Walk By Night* (1949).

The dextrous Cape Town Castle Ghost, which has been appearing in South Africa for almost three hundred years

CARNACKI THE GHOST FINDER

In company with Algernon Blackwood's John Silence, Carnacki the Ghost Finder is perhaps the supreme psychic detective in supernatural fiction. The creation of William Hope Hodgson (1877–1918), Carnacki is a "ghost breaker" as well as a ghost-hunter, and the best short stories featuring him have been collected together as *Carnacki, The Ghost Finder*, first published in 1913 and constantly reprinted. Hope Hodgson was a remarkably talented writer on the supernatural who is only belatedly receiving the acclaim that he deserves—and this is despite the fact that during his ill-fated life he was described by the *Liverpool Courier* as "probably our best writer of ghost stories, whether he finds them afloat or ashore." Among his outstanding tales of the supernatural at sea should be mentioned "The Mystery of the Derelict" (1907), "The Voice in the Night" (1907) and his novel *The Ghost Pirates* (1909). Hope Hodgson was killed tragically while on active service in the First World War.

CASSIO BURROUGHS'S TWO PHANTOMS

The strange story of the haunting of Cassio Burroughs is one of the most bizarre episodes in the whole history of the supernatural. Burroughs was apparently a dissolute and rather wild man-about-town who lived in London during the middle years of the seventeenth century. According to the legend he was on his way to fight a duel one evening when his path took him across a graveyard. There he was suddenly confronted by not one, but *two* ghosts, according to Lionel A. Weatherley, who recounts the episode in his book *The Supernatural* (1933). "The one was the ghost of a beautiful Italian lady whom he had wronged and deserted, and who died broken-hearted. On the other hand was a grinning skeleton—omen of his coming death." Panic-stricken, the man fled from the graveyard, but could not avoid the duel which all too prophetically ended fatally for him. No sooner had news of Burroughs's death begun to spread over London than his encounter with the two spirits became a major topic of conversation and was soon being broadcast still further afield in ballads and broadsheets. The illustration on page 26 is taken from one typical penny version of his meeting with the phantoms. Another account of the events is to be found in Aubrey's *Miscellanies* (1696).

CATS

Cats are the most common form of animal phenomena to be found in haunted houses, according to an article "Cats and the Unknown" by Elliott O'Donnell in the *Occult Review* of December 1962. The tradition of ghostly felines goes back to the time of the ancient Egyptians when cats were worshipped as gods, says Mr. O'Donnell, and tradition has also asserted that the Devil himself can assume the shape of a cat. He continues:

Cassio Burroughs, the man-about-town whose death was predicted by two phantoms in the seventeenth century

> There are, at the present moment, many houses in England haunted by phantasms in the form of black cats, of so sinister and hostile an appearance, that one can only assume that unless they are the actual spirits of cats, earthbound through cruel and vicious propensities, they must be vice-elementals, i.e., spirits that have never inhabited any material body, and which have either been generated by vicious thoughts, or else have been attracted elsewhere to a spot by some crime or vicious act once perpetrated there. Vice-elemental is merely the modern name for fiend or demon.

The ghosts of cats are also discussed by Raymond Bayless in *Animal Ghosts* (1970).

CATTLE

The curious story of ghostly cattle that can be heard but never seen in the Gippsland Hills to the south of Yallourn in Australia has puzzled ghost-hunters for years. The haunting seems to date from the middle of the last century when a famous stampede of cattle nearly destroyed the small town of Moe. No sign of the drovers who were supposed to be looking after this herd was ever found, and even when cattlemen from the district went out to round up the animals, they only succeeded in recapturing a small percentage of those which had been seen charging through the town. Ever since then, says the legend, drovers in the Gippsland Hills have heard sounds of ghostly cattle on the move—but not once have they been able to catch sight of even a single cow.

CAULD LAD OF HILTON

Half-ghost and half-goblin, the Cauld lad of Hilton is a strange spirit that has been repeatedly seen in the Durham, England area. He is supposed to be the spirit of a stable-boy named Roger Skelton who was brutally killed in 1609 by Robert Hilton, owner of Hilton Castle. He now apparently interferes in human affairs by making a mess in kitchens and generally untidying houses. The Cauld Lad's activities are somewhat like those of a poltergeist. His story is told in detail in Robert Surtees's *History of the County of Durham* (1816).

CHAGRIN

The chagrin, which is also sometimes referred to as the cogrino or harginn, is a gypsy word for a particular type of evil ghost. According to *A Survey of the Occult* edited by Julian Franklyn (1935) the spirit is most often seen in the form of a large yellow hedgehog and is invariably an omen of some kind of disaster to follow.

CHINESE GHOSTS

Despite the great upheaval in Chinese society this century, a great many of the people still cling to the old beliefs in ghosts, dividing them into two main categories, the shen, or good spirits, and the kuei, or evil spirits. The shen are the ancestral ghosts and so deserving of veneration, while the kuei are connected with darkness, misfortune and death. According to G. W. Mead in *Chinese Ghouls and Goblins* (1928) there are "perhaps twenty distinct varieties of ghosts and demons, and hundreds of sub-varieties not always easily distinguishable one from another." Mead says the Chinese are not afraid of their ghosts—they welcome the shen, and will boldly face up to the evil kuei with weapons of iron or steel, which the spirits are said to fear. The mandarins and Confucian scholars were once believed to have power over the kuei, but nowadays any intelligent person can outwit them, for they are said to be invariably foolish. Like the people in the West, the Chinese attempt to make contact with their shen by means of divination, using a planchette of their own design. Of this, Mead writes,

> The Chinese instrument consists of a V-shaped twig, something like a European divining-rod, with the difference that another twig is fixed in the point of the V at right angles to it, so that when the bifurcated stick is taken

A hill spirit, one of the multitude of Chinese ghosts still widely believed in by the population

> horizontally in two hands, the "pencil" is vertical. It is held over a tray of sand, and as the characters are traced they are copied down on a sheet of paper. A domestic planchette is also arranged by inverting a sieve over a plate containing flour, and pushing a chopstick through the mesh.

Mead says that ectoplasmic materializations were known in China hundreds of years B.C., and there are also professional spirit mediums, known as wu, who are usually women. They are not, he adds, generally regarded with much favor by the population, who appear to prefer their own direct contact with ghosts.

CHRISTMAS DAY

Although Christmas has always been regarded as the special time of the year for ghosts, a widespread superstition held by many people says that the spirits of the dead are specifically prohibited from appearing on Christmas Day. No doubt so as not to spoil the fun!

CIDEVILLE CASE

The ghostly activities that were recorded in 1850 in the parsonage of Cideville in Normandy have been described as probably the most varied of any single poltergeist. Thirty-four witnesses were to testify about the disturbances, which were first revealed when a man named Felix Thorel brought the village priest of Cideville, Father Tinel, to court for defaming his character by calling him a witch. The Father had made this accusation because he believed Thorel to be the cause of all the strange noises and activities in his home. The case is recorded by Sacheverell Sitwell in his book *Poltergeists* (1940), in which he observes that the case contains almost every category of poltergeist phenomenon: knockings, rapping of popular tunes, tables and furniture being moved, knives thrown, desks rising and falling, stones thrown, wind rushing, and pillows and bed coverings snatched away. Despite intensive investigation, the case has never been satisfactorily resolved.

COCK CROW

According to an old superstition found throughout the world, when a cock crows at daybreak this is a sign that all ghosts must return to the underworld where they spend the daylight hours.

COCK LANE GHOST

The haunting of the Cock Lane Ghost in 1762 was a London sensation in its time and has retained its fame to this day. The tiny terraced house in the narrow lane where the manifestations took place proved a magnet for the curious, and people literally fought to get into the small room where a twelve-year-old girl named Elizabeth Parsons relayed weird and frightening messages from the ghost. The spirit claimed to be Frances Lynes and she accused her lover, William Kent, of murdering her by poison while she lay sick of the smallpox. Because of the strange noises she made, the phantom became known as "Scratching Fanny," and little Elizabeth described her as "a shrouded figure without hands." Such was the interest in the events that several notable people visited the "house of mystery" as it was called, including Dr. Samuel Johnson (who came with an investigating committee but neither saw nor heard anything), the Duke of York, Horace Walpole, and Oliver Goldsmith who anonymously wrote the first account of the haunting, *The Mystery Revealed*, published that same year and illustrated here. Although the child was later exposed as a fraud, this did not explain all the incidents that had occurred in what has been seen by some authorities as a rare instance in which a ghost actually ventured into the open in search of revenge. The Cock Lane Ghost was also made famous by William Hogarth's print ridiculing the public's credulity. Two notable studies of the event are *Cock Lane and Common Sense* by Andrew Lang (1894) and *The Cock Lane Ghost* by Douglas Grant (1965).

THE

MYSTERY REVEALED;

Containing a SERIES of

TRANSACTIONS

AND

AUTHENTIC TESTIMONIALS,

Respecting the supposed

COCK-LANE GHOST;

Which have hitherto been concealed from the PUBLIC.

—— *Since none the Living dare implead,*
Arraign him in the Person of the Dead.

DRYDEN.

LONDON:

Printed for W. BRISTOW, in St. Paul's Church-yard; and C. ETHRINGTON, York.

MDCCXLII.

An account of the famous Cock Lane Ghost written by Oliver Goldsmith

COLLINS, WILLIAM WILKIE (1824–89)

Wilkie Collins was another writer from the Victorian era whose stories of the supernatural have proved timeless and enduring, in particular "A Terribly Strange Bed" (1852), "The Dead Hand" (1857) and his splendid ghost novel,

Wilkie Collins, ghost-story writer and friend of Charles Dickens

The Haunted Hotel (1877). Collins is also famous as the friend and collaborator of Charles Dickens, and the author of two classic detective novels, *The Woman in White* (1860) and *The Moonstone* (1868).

COOK, FLORENCE (1856–1904)

Florence Cook is famous as the medium who not only raised a ghost spirit named Katie King but also allowed her to be photographed—an example being the picture here taken in 1874. Miss Cook was said to have been interested in the supernatural from her childhood, attended her first seance when barely a teenager, and began producing her own materializations at the age of just fifteen! The famous spirit she raised, Katie King, was said to be the

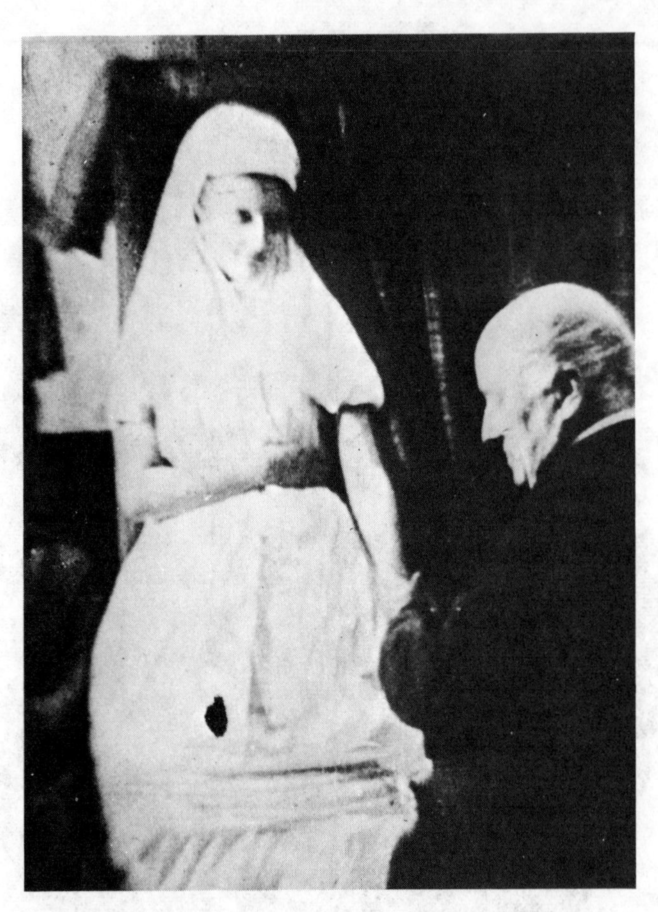

The medium Florence Cook is said to have raised this spirit, Katie King, at her seances

daughter of John King, an alias for Sir Henry Morgan (1635–88), the British buccaneer who later became the Lieutenant-Governor of Jamaica. Although many people claimed the materialization to be fraudulent (that it was Florence Cook herself in disguise), her case was constantly espoused by the great physicist Sir William Crookes, who claimed to have seen the two women quite separately. The curious story of Florence Cook and Katie King is related by J. A. Hill in his *Spiritualism: Its History, Phenomena and Doctrine* (1918).

CORPSE BIRD

The derwyn corph is a peculiarly Welsh phantom, which is widely known as the "corpse bird." This eerie, frightening bird is an omen of death when it appears, and it usually sits on the windowsill of a room where someone is going to die and taps harshly against the glass. Elliott O'Donnell describes the corpse bird in his book *Family Ghosts and Ghostly Phenomena* (1933).

CORPSE CANDLES

The canhywallan cyrth, or corpse candle, is perhaps the best-known of Welsh phantoms. These strange lights are called candles because their shapes resemble that of a candle flame, and they are said to appear in the vicinity of a house just before someone is about to die. According to T. Charley in *News from the Invisible World* (1896), it is possible to discern from the corpse candle whether the person about to die will be young or old. If the light is small and pale blue in color, then the death will be that of a child; while if it is large and ruddy, then it will be an adult in the prime of life. Should the light be large in size, and either pale blue or white, then this signifies the death of someone who is old and has been ill for some time. Welsh history is full of accounts of the canhywallan cyrth, a striking example being quoted by Charley in his *News from the Invisible World*:

> The Reverend Mr. Davis has given me an account of the Corpse Candle. "Of late," he writes, "my sexton's wife, an aged, understanding woman, saw from her bed a little bluish candle upon the table end; within two or three days after comes a fellow in, enquiring for her husband, and, taking something from under his cloak, clapt it down directly upon the table end, where she had seen the candle; and what was it but a dead-born child."

CO-WALKER

The co-walker is the Scottish equivalent of a doppelgänger: a spirit that exactly matches a man or woman as he or she is in life. According to tradition they first appear not long before a person's death, and have a habit of appearing again at funerals, terrifying all who see them. They are described in Robert Kirk's book, *The Secret Commonwealth* (1815).

CRAWFORD, FRANCIS MARION (1854–1909)

After years of neglect, F. Marion Crawford is at last being recognized as one of the great writers of supernatural fiction—and this is surely only appropriate as one of his tales, "The Upper Berth" is widely regarded as the most reprinted of all ghost stories. Indeed, two others of Crawford's ghost stories, "The Screaming Skull" and "The Dead Smile" are also popular with anthologists—and his seems a classic case of a man's work being better known than the man himself! Although generally thought to be an American, Crawford was actually born in Italy and spent much of his youth in the Orient where he became fascinated with mysticism. He wrote over forty books during his lifetime, but it was the little group of supernatural stories gathered together as *Wandering Ghosts* and published posthumously in 1911 that kept his name alive among a small band of enthusiasts and has subsequently played a major part in establishing his importance in the genre.

CREWE CIRCLE

The Crewe Circle was the name given to a group of spirit photographers led by a man named William Hope (1863–1933) and based in Crewe, England. In 1905, Hope claimed to be able to take photographs of the souls of people who had died, and so convincing were his pictures that he soon gathered around him others who said they were similarly gifted. In the years that followed, the products of the Crewe Circle were investigated by numerous societies and individuals, including the Royal Photographic Society and Sir Arthur Conan Doyle, who was so impressed with their work that he wrote a book mostly about the circle called *The Case for Spirit Photography* (1922). Conan Doyle himself posed with the members for a photograph taken by William Hope, and afterwards professed himself amazed at the result—although the ghost face that materialized on the print did appear sideways! Of Hope he later said,

> That he has been fiercely attacked goes without saying, but each fresh allegation against him has ended in smoke, while his gifts have grown stronger with time. No medium can ever honestly guarantee success, but it would probably be within the mark if one claimed that Hope attained it three times out of five, though the results vary much in visibility and value.

Recent research into those spirit photographs that have not definitely been proved fakes has led to the suggestion that they might be the result of spontaneous images on the film plates. See the discussion by John Michell and Robert J. M. Rickard in their book, *Phenomena* (1977).

A photograph of the Crewe Circle to which Sir Arthur Conan Doyle belonged. The "spirit face" that allegedly appeared on the negative can be seen by turning the book sideways!

William Crookes, the chemist and physicist who became fascinated with the supernatural and was photographed with the spirit of Katie King

CROOKES, SIR WILLIAM (1832–1919)

Although he is perhaps best known as a much honored chemist and physicist, Sir William Crookes was profoundly interested in all aspects of the supernatural, spiritualism in particular, and it is claimed that he attended more seances than any other scientifically qualified investigator both before his time or since. During these seances he witnessed the materialization of numerous human forms, and a photograph still exists (reproduced here) of him with the spirit known as Katie King, who was repeatedly raised by the medium Florence Cook. Crookes was also a member, and for a time President, of The Ghost Club in London, and took a great interest in the many hauntings reported to this organization. Throughout his life, Crookes believed in the possibility of many aspects of the supernatural, and although skeptics have poured scorn on certain of his opinions, his massive work, *Researches in the Phenomena of Spiritualism,* assembled posthumously in 1926, is required reading for any serious researcher into the field.

CROSSROAD GHOSTS

Crossroads have long been held as a place where hauntings take place, although the reasons for this belief have never been easy to explain. Some interesting suggestions are offered by ghost-hunter Elliott O'Donnell in his book *Haunted Britain* (1948):

> Some think it is because in olden times murderers, sorcerers and suicides were buried at cross-roads, with a stake thrust through them in a foolishly vain attempt to keep their spirits from wandering; others think it is because witches and wizards were believed to hold orgies and practise the Black Art at cross-roads; while others, again, think cross-roads, like lonely pools, old quarries and some woods, have a peculiar attraction for a certain species of spirits.

Several examples of haunted crossroads are given in the Reverend Frederick Lee's *More Glimpses of the World Unseen* (1878).

CROWE, CATHERINE (1800–70)

Mrs. Crowe was the author of an early and still important study of apparitions called *The Night Side of Nature* (1848), in which she published the results of years of enquiry into the supernatural. She was known to have had a morbid and rather despondent nature and it has been suggested that her excessive indulgence into the macabre brought about her brief period of insanity. Despite this, her book displays a remarkably scientific approach to the subject of ghosts and has proved a model for much that has subsequently been written.

DAVENPORT BROTHERS

Ira and William Davenport were two American mediums who between 1860 and 1880 astounded audiences on both sides of the Atlantic by apparently materializing "spirit hands" that untied difficult knots and played musical instruments. Such was the style with which the brothers put on their act that many spiritualists believed they were aided by ghosts, and although professional magicians were able to show that everything they did was just a conjuring trick, their reputation remained remarkably high. In the advertising literature for their performances, the brothers boasted:

An amusing contemporary engraving of Ira and William Davenport with the "spirit hands," which enabled them to carry out their fraudulent act

> Musical instruments are made to play in the most extraordinary manner, and in the most profound and mysterious way. Human hands and arms become visible, and many other interesting experiments are presented, originating only with the Davenport Brothers in the year 1855 and never produced with success by imitators. Sceptics are specially invited to be present and occupy front seats!

According to Julian Franklyn in *A Survey of the Occult* (1835), "They were exposed by a Lancashire weaver who knew how to tie a 'Tom Fool' knot. This they were unable to loosen, hence they remained bound and the 'spirits' gave no musical performance."

DEATH

The phenomenon of ghosts of dying people being seen by friends or relatives at a far distant point has been discussed in numerous works, notably the monumental study *Phantasm of the Living* by Frederic W. H. Myers, Edmund Gurney, and Frank Podmore (1886). Commenting on these occurrences, the Scottish mythologist Andrew Lang has said, "the number of hallucinations corresponding with death or some other crisis is far too great to be regarded as merely casual." In this writer's opinion, the most striking account of this phenomenon occurs in the book *Falling Through Space* by Richard Hillary. Hillary was an RAF pilot during the Second World War and while convalescing in a British hospital, saw, as he lay in bed, a vision of a close friend and fellow pilot, Peter Pease, being killed in an aerial fight with a German Messerschmitt. It was not until two days later that it could be confirmed that Pease had, in fact, died at the precise moment Hillary had his vision.

One of the popular Victorian fake spirit photographs apparently showing the ghost of the departed mingling with the mourners at a funeral!

DEATH SOUND

The cyhyraeth, or death sound, is another specifically Welsh phenomenon which haunts a number of the country's oldest families. It is a disembodied wailing or moaning noise heard immediately before someone's death. Reports of this indescribably sad sound have recently been reported in the area of the River Towy, and these have helped the continuation of the legend.

DEE, JOHN (1527–1608)

John Dee, described as "Queen Elizabeth's Merlin" and famous for his powers as a magician, his enormous library of books on arcane subjects and his great knowledge of occult matters, is today best remembered because of a famous illustration (reproduced over) which shows him raising a ghost. The affair has always been shrouded in some mystery because his companion on this occasion was a renowned charlatan named Edward Kelly who had already duped Dee on a number of occasions. Nevertheless, it is known that in 1581 at a place called Wootton-in-the Dale in Lancashire, the two men employed the art of necromancy to try and contact a ghost. Later in his life, Dee claimed to have regularly conversed with ghosts and spirits and he left a record of this entitled *A True and Faithful Relation of What Passed for Many Years between Dr. J. Dee and Some Spirits*, which was later published by Meric Casaubon. Dee and his world are examined in detail in Frances A. Yates's splendid study, *The Occult Philosophy in the Elizabethan Age* (1979).

John Dee and his partner Edward Kelly raising a ghost in the churchyard at Wootton-in-the-Dale in 1581

DEMON OF SPREYTON

The Demon of Spreyton was a famous eighteenth-century poltergeist featured in Richard Bovet's important book on demonology, *Pandaemonium* (1684). Bovet (1641–*c.*1703) divided this work into two halves, the first concerned with witchcraft and the second with fifteen ghost stories he had collected and researched—of which "The Demon of Spreyton" is the most fascinating. Bovet was a believer in apparitions as he confessed: "The more unaccountable these things seem to be in themselves (the real matter of fact being proved) it ought the more to prevail toward a belief of these extraordinary agencies." Andrew Lang has retold the fascinating story of the Demon of Spreyton for modern readers in his *Cock Lane and Common Sense* (1894).

DEVIL OF HJALTA-STAD

The legend of the Devil of Hjalta-Stad is one of the most famous ghost stories in Scandinavia. This weird, semi-naked figure that suddenly appeared in the little Swedish community of Hjalta-Stad in 1750 was seen by several dozen people and created such a panic that many of the villagers immediately fled from their homes. The bald-headed phantom was apparently recognized as a villager who had been ostracized by the local people for some unknown crime and had vowed on his deathbed that he would return to haunt his persecutors. Why he should have returned in a shroud when he had been buried in funeral clothes was not certain, but the ghost created havoc in the district for some days until the local clergyman exorcized both the house where the man had lived and the spot where he was buried. After this the Devil of Hjalta-Stad, as the phantom had become known, disappeared and life returned to normal. There have, however, been reports that the spirit has been seen again since, still as malevolent and half-dressed as before.

DICKENS, CHARLES (1812–70)

Charles Dickens is, of course, the author of perhaps the most famous ghost story of all, *A Christmas Carol* (1843) in which the ghosts of past, present and future combine to make the old miser, Ebenezer Scrooge, change his ways. The success of this story started Dickens on his tradition of producing a ghost story each Christmas, and he also encouraged the contributors to his magazines, *Household Words* and later *All The Year Round*, to come up with similar spooky stories each festive season—a tradition still very much practiced today. Among his own notable contributions to the genre are "The Haunted Man" (1848) and "The Haunted House" (1859), as well as "No. 1 Branch Line: The Signalman," his superb and much reprinted short ghost story. Perhaps not surprisingly, Charles Dickens himself has been seen as a ghost—firstly near the Corn Exchange in Rochester which he immortalized in *The Mystery of Edwin Drood* (1870) and also in the vicinity of the old

The Devil of Hjalta-Stad, the gruesome and terrifying Scandinavian ghost, which appeared in 1750

burial ground of St. Nicholas where he had expressed a desire to be buried. The great author was, in fact, laid to rest in Westminster Abbey, but this has apparently not prevented his shade from returning to the town he loved so much during his lifetime.

DOGS

Phantom dogs are reported all over the British Isles, such as the famous Mauthe Dog that haunts Peel Castle on the Isle of Man, the terrifying gwyilgi in Wales, the trash or striker in Lancashire, as well as the north-country barguest. Writing about these apparitions in his book, *Animal Ghosts* (1913), Elliott O'Donnell says, "As to what class of spirits the spectre dog belongs, that is impossible to say. At the most we can only surmise, and I should think the chances of its being the actual phantasm of some dead dog or an elemental are about equal." Mr. O'Donnell believes that living dogs have the power to see ghosts and they indicate the fact by howling dismally. "In my opinion," he writes, "there is very little doubt that dogs actually see some kind of phantasm that, knowing when death is about to take place, visits the house of the doomed and stands beside his, or her, couch. I have had this phantasm described to me, by those who declare they have seen it, as a very tall, hooded

"Redlaw and the Phantom," a famous illustration by J. Leech for Charles Dickens's story, "The Haunted Man"

figure, clad in a dark, loose-flowing costume—its face never discernible." Mr. O'Donnell maintains that a dog is an essential companion for any ghost-hunter. "When I investigate a haunted house, I generally take a dog with me, because experience has taught me that a dog seldom fails to give notice, in some way or another—either by whining, or growling, or crouching shivering at one's feet, or springing on one's lap and trying to bury its head in one's coat—of the proximity of a ghost."

DOMOVOY

Domovoy is the popular Russian term for a ghost. These spirits are rather like poltergeists in that they tend to make a noise and generally disturb people. However, they will also do household chores while the family is asleep if they have been treated with respect.

DOPPELGÄNGER

Doppelgänger is the German expression for a ghost that is actually the "double" or identical likeness of somebody who is still alive. The spirit appears to haunt that person and by so doing indicates that he or she may soon expect some terrible tragedy to befall him or her. These ghosts are also known in Scotland, where they are called the "co-walkers," and in a famous old book, *The Secret Commonwealth* by Robert Kirk (1691) they are described as "in every way like the Man, as a Twin-brother and Companion, haunting him as his shadow, both before and after the original is dead."

DOWNING STREET GHOST

Number 10 Downing Street, the residence of the British Prime Minister, has long been said to be haunted, though no occupant has reported seeing the ghost for some years. According to the legend, the figure is dressed in Regency-style clothes and gives the appearance of having been a man of authority, perhaps even a Prime Minister of that period. The ghost apparently has a very benevolent look on its face and only shows itself at times of national crisis. The last recorded sighting was in 1960 when workmen carrying out renovations at the back of the house saw a strangely old-fashioned figure, rather misty white, moving across the garden.

DOYLE, SIR ARTHUR CONAN (1859–1930)

Although world-famous as the creator of the immortal detective, Sherlock Holmes, Sir Arthur Conan Doyle was profoundly interested in all aspects of the supernatural, and became such a strong advocate of the cause of spiritualism that he devoted much of the later part of his life to promoting its cause. With hindsight it is possible to see that he was cruelly deluded by certain unscrupulous people and that many of the cases of paranormal phenomena which he reported were fraudulent. He attended numerous seances, was allegedly put in touch with the spirit of his dead mother, and heard the voice of his son, killed in the First World War. He also championed the work of a group of spirit photographers known as the Crewe Circle whom he wrote about in his book *The Case for Spirit Photography* (1922). Because his introduction to the supernatural had come through his friendship with a member of The Ghost Club in London in 1887, he was always interested in stories of hauntings and actually visited a number of haunted houses. (By a curious twist, Sir Arthur's old home, the rambling Windlesham Manor in Sussex, is now said to be haunted by *his* ghost!) Despite the ridicule to which he was frequently subjected, Conan Doyle remained convinced of a life after death and the possibility of making contact with spirits, and cited two instances in his autobiography, *Memories and Adventures* (1924), which time has been unable to disprove. On one occasion he received messages through

An alleged spirit photograph of Sir Arthur Conan Doyle, who devoted many years to promoting spiritualism. The photograph is a crude fake

the mediumship of his second wife containing details that she could not possibly have known, and on the other personally experienced a ghost in a haunted house. "In the middle of the night," he wrote, "a fearsome uproar broke out and made no impression upon the threads we had stretched across the doors and windows." When this house was later burned down and the skeleton of a child was discovered, Sir Arthur believed it had been her spirit that was responsible for the disturbances. Conan Doyle utilized his knowledge of the supernatural in a good deal of his fiction—in particular in short-story collections like *Dreamland and Ghostland* (1886) and *The Last Gallery* (1911). He also recounted a number of his psychic experiences in the last book to appear before his death, *The Edge of the Unknown* (1930).

DRAKE'S DRUM

One of the most curious ghost stories of the sea is associated with a rather ordinary looking drum that is kept in the Plymouth City Museum in England. This was the drum that Sir Francis Drake (*c.* 1540–96) took with him on his voyage around the world, and which is said to have the power to summon back his ghost from the dead if he is needed to save his beloved

England from attack. According to the legend, as Sir Francis lay dying he said that if anyone beat on the drum when England was in danger, he would return and lead his country to victory. With the passage of time this legend has been varied somewhat, and it is now said that the drum will sound of its *own* accord if England is about to be attacked! Instances of this happening in both the First and Second World Wars as well as the general history of the drum are recounted by Raymond Lamont Brown in *Phantoms of the Sea* (1972).

DRUDE

The drude is an old English expression for a nightmare fiend. According to several authorities, a young witch became a drude when she reached the age of forty and then had the power to haunt any victim with terrible visions.

DRUMMER OF THE AIRLIES

The Phantom Drummer of Cortachy is one of the most widely known ghosts in Scotland and has been the subject of innumerable reports and stories. The legend concerns a handsome young drummer who foolishly made love to the wife of the Earl of Airlie who lived at Cortachy Castle. Caught in the act, the drummer was thrust into his drum, and thrown from the battlements. Ever since then the spirit of the young man has returned from time to time to haunt the ancient castle, banging his drum defiantly and loudly enough to waken the dead. Certain reports say that after every one of his visitations a member of the Airlie family had died. A full account of the legend and the more recent reports of the drummer are to be found in *Haunted Houses and Family Legends* by John Ingram (1907).

DRUMMER OF TEDWORTH

The story of the Phantom Drummer of Tedworth was certainly the most famous ghost story of the seventeenth century, and has subsequently been referred to as "one of the earliest well-attested poltergeist cases in England" by Harry Price in *Poltergeist Over England* (1945). The events took place in the small country town of Tedworth (now Tidworth) in Wiltshire when there was a sudden outbreak of drumming sounds in the house of the local magistrate, Mr. John Mompesson. Children were lifted into the air, shoes were flung at a man's head, chamber-pots were emptied on to beds and a horse had one of its rear legs forced into its mouth. Mompesson, a sober, conscientious and well-respected man, was just one of many witnesses to these phenomena, which first occurred in the spring of 1661 and continued for exactly a year. The events began in March when an itinerant conjuror and one-time regimental drummer, William Drury, was arrested for obtaining money with forged documents. He was brought before Magistrate Mompes-

The famous Drummer of Tedworth—a contemporary illustration of the baffling seventeenth-century haunting

son, who decided to let him off with a warning, but confiscated his drum and told him to leave the district. Almost immediately afterwards the drumming sounds commenced; witnesses reported seeing the drum rise in the air inside Mr. Mompesson's house and give off booming sounds. After several nights of this, the sleepless magistrate had it broken up; but the following night the sounds continued unabated, this time above the house, and the other strange manifestations also began to be seen. Those who naturally suspected that the vagrant Drury had secretly returned and was to blame were soon proved wrong, for the man had been arrested for theft in Gloucester and sentenced to transportation. Stories of the drummer soon spread throughout the country, and one of the first people to come to investigate was Joseph Glanvill, chaplain to Charles II and author of a famous book on the supernatural, *Sadducismus Triumphatus* (1681). He heard the drumming "usually five nights together . . . on the outside of the house which is most of it board" and collected eyewitness accounts from children and servants. A committee subsequently appointed by the King to enquire into the case could deduce no human agency. Late in 1662 the drumming ceased as suddenly and mysteriously as it had begun—but the story of the poltergeist believed to have caused it has continued to be studied to this day.

DUENDA DE ZARAGOZA

The tale of the Duenda de Zaragoza is one of the best known Spanish ghost stories and it created widespread interest throughout Europe in 1934. In the November of that year a strange voice began to be heard speaking down a stove pipe in the house occupied by a family named Palazon in the town of Saragossa. When the family reported this, numerous local officials, including doctors and policemen, visited the house, and were soon holding conversations with the "voice," which not only spoke but also answered a variety of questions. It called itself the "Duenda de Zaragoza" and displayed a remarkable intelligence and wit. At first the family's sixteen-year-old servant girl, Maria Pascuela, was suspected of being the voice, but a carefully staged enquiry conducted by the police and the local magistrate, established there was no direct link and the only possibility concerning her was that she might have achieved the effect by "unconscious ventriloquism." In any event, in December 1934, the ghost voice spoke its final lines and was never heard from again. The mystery of Saragossa has remained unsolved to this day and is discussed in Nandor Fodor's *The Saragossa Ghost* (1935).

DUNCAN, HELEN (1898–1956)

Mrs. Helen Duncan was perhaps the most extraordinary of all British mediums, and during a career that was studded with controversy, she was actually sent to prison in 1932 as a result of being convicted on a charge brought under the Witchcraft Act, now mercifully repealed. It was alleged that during a seance she had apparently materialized a spirit from the dead, which was then dramatically seized by one of the sitters and proved to be Mrs. Duncan herself. In another famous case investigated by Harry Price, Mrs. Duncan appeared to materialize another spirit, but this proved to be made of cheesecloth as a photograph, secretly taken (and reprinted over), clearly revealed. The "spirit" was thereafter rather unkindly referred to as "the coat-hanger witch"!

DUPPY

The duppy is a West Indian ghost who can be summoned by a secret ritual to do the caller's bidding. Part of this rite involves throwing some coins and a glass of rum on a grave, and this will bring out the ghostly shade who is understandably in such a bad temper that he will play any evil trick he is asked! According to the old tradition, the duppy is the personification of the evil in man, and although he can only operate at night and must return to his former dwelling in the grave before dawn, if he is prevented from doing this for any reason then he will never be able to harm any living person again. The West Indians say that if a duppy breathes on a person then he or she will be violently ill, while anybody touched by the spirit will suffer a fit. The best

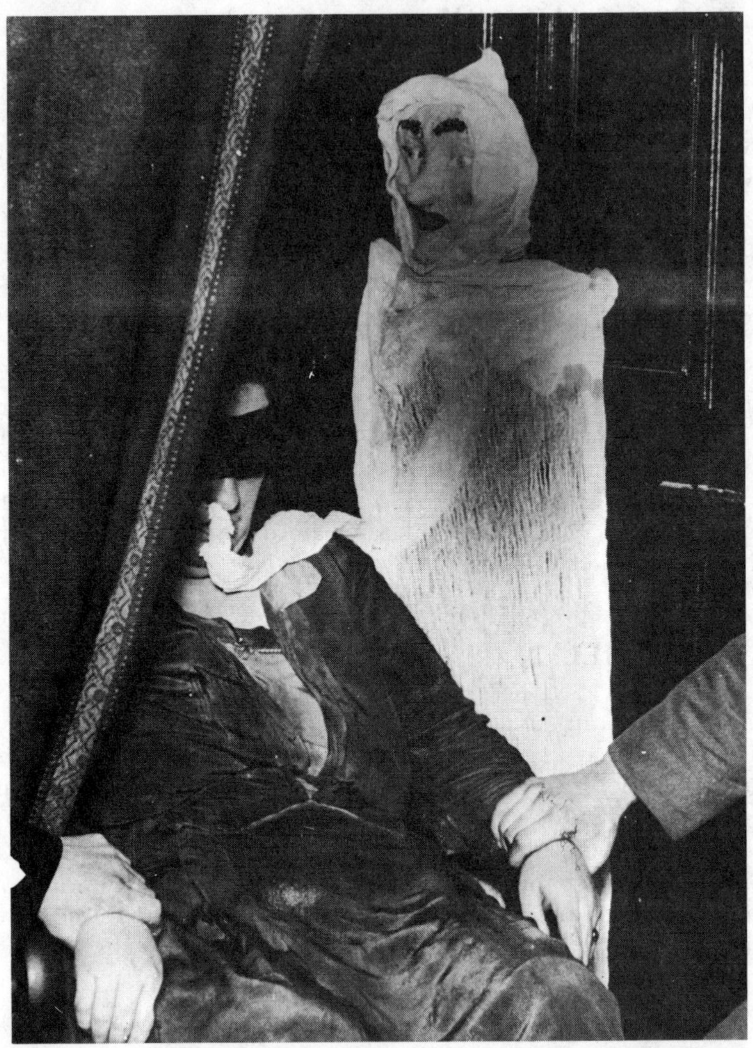

Mrs. Helen Duncan allegedly materializing a spirit—as a result of this photograph showing it to be made of cheescloth the ghost became known as "the coat-hanger witch"!

way to keep them at bay, according to an old belief, is to place tobacco seeds—which they hate—around the doors and windows of the home. The duppy is discussed in detail in Zora Hurston's *Voodoo Gods* (1939).

E

ECTOPLASM

Ectoplasm, or teleplasm as it is sometimes called, is a strange substance that is said to be extruded from the mouth, ears, nostrils, or genitals of certain mediums while in a trance, and materializes into all or part of a human form. It has been variously described as looking like white chiffon, paper, cheese-cloth, eggwhite or even animal lung-tissue, and derives its name from the Greek words *ektos* and *plasma*, meaning exteriorized substance. Describing ectoplasm in *A Survey of the Occult* (1935), S. G. Soal writes

> Some observers describe it as being inert while others declare that it squirms and wriggles. It is said to be plastic, to mould itself into hands and heads and even into the complete forms of animals and human beings. It can also organise itself into rigid rods which are used to produce loud raps and into cantilevers which support heavy tables in the air. In fact, the variety of its functions is as amazing as the alterations in its appearance. It is a most chameleon-like form of matter. And, strange to say, all mediums who produce it are sooner or later accused of fraud.

On the other hand, the German investigator, Baron Albert von Schrenck-Notzing, who claimed to have examined a sample of the substance in his laboratory, declared it to be "a sort of transitory matter which originates in the organism in a manner unknown to us and possesses unknown biological functions and formative possibilities." Perhaps the most famous example of

An extraordinary photograph of ectoplasm being produced by the American medium Mrs. Margery Crandon

a medium who apparently regularly produced ectoplasm was the American Mrs. Margery Crandon (1887–1941), who, though denounced as a fraud, materialized the phenomenon at a closely controlled experiment in 1924 attended by leading psychical researchers and the ultra-skeptical investigator and escapologist, Harry Houdini. Her story is fully related in *Margery the Medium* by Malcolm J. Bird (1925).

EDGEHILL BATTLE

The first major battle of the English Civil War was fought at Edgehill in Warwickshire on October 23, 1642, when the Parliamentarians led by the Earl of Essex faced the Royalists under King Charles I. The battle proved indecisive, and might well have rapidly lost its importance but for a totally inexplicable event that occurred two months later. For on December 23, shortly after midnight, a group of shepherds and travellers in the vicinity of the battlefield saw the entire engagement fought all over again by two phantom armies in the sky! The amazingly detailed account of the cut and thrust of the fighting that they were later to give to investigators matched exactly the accounts recorded by survivors of the original battle. The story is recorded by Joseph Glanvill in his *Sadducismus Triumphatus,* written in 1682.

ELECTRIC HORROR OF BERKELEY SQUARE

The house numbered 50 in London's fashionable Berkeley Square was once reputed to be haunted by an eerie ghost known as the "electric horror," and it also had the distinction of having inspired Sir Edward Bulwer-Lytton (1803–73) to write his classic story "The Haunted and the Haunters," pub-

A sketch of the "electric horror" of Berkeley Square, London, from Elliott O'Donnell's *Ghosts* (1959)

lished in 1859. (The story is alternatively known as "The House and the Brain" and has been described by the American H. P. Lovecraft as "one of the best short haunted-house tales ever written.") Number 50 Berkeley Square was formerly the home of George Canning, and the first reports that it was haunted by a grim and noisy spirit were made in the early 1850s. Apart from the strange noises, the ghost also threw things about and smashed windows—and, as if this was not enough, several occupants of the premises complained that "the very party walls of the house, when touched, are found saturated with electric horror": which gave the ghost its name. Despite the many reports of this phantom, claims were also advanced that the strange noises were actually man-made—by a group of forgers who surreptitiously used the premises and created the strange noises to keep the inquisitive away while they made dud coins! In any event, the legend about the building persisted, and for many years it was a favorite tourist attraction for visitors to London, according to Harry Price who recounts the story in detail in his book *Poltergeist Over England* (1945).

ELECTRIZERS

According to the American medium John M. Spear, in 1854, "the electrizers" was the name given to a group of ghostly spirits who had told him they were prepared to communicate the principle of life to mankind. Writing of this ludicrous episode in *A Survey of the Occult* (1935) S. G. Soal says,

> The Electrizers intended to communicate the principle of life to a machine made of copper and zinc which was to be worked by spiritual energy and which was to revolutionise human life on our planet. In order to effect this desirable consummation, the friends of the medium constructed some kind of mechanical device of copper and zinc. A woman was found and she experienced imaginary pangs of child-labour, but the machine refused to come to life. In spite of all efforts it refused to budge, and was ultimately wrecked by an angry mob which broke into the building in which it was housed!

ELEMENTALS

Elementals are among the most bizarre of all ghosts, for they are supposed to be supernatural beings who have never been human, rather than the spirits of people who once lived. Such beings are recorded from the very earliest times, and many of our fairy tales and legends grew up from stories about them. Elementals usually take the form of strange, glowing lights, sometimes roughly human-shaped, which appear where tragedies have occurred. They have also been reported in the likeness of peculiar birds and animals, and as their haunts are near treacherous marshes and shifting sands they should be avoided at all costs. A well-known story often associated with elementals comes from North Carolina where a stretch of railway line on which a man was decapitated by a train is haunted by a round, eerie, white light. According to local lore the light is the dead man's head searching in vain for his body.

ELIZABETH I (1533–1603)

Queen Elizabeth I, the "Virgin Queen," was said to have been psychic and just before her death she had a vision in which she saw herself lying pale and shrivelled on her bed. This omen apparently led to her rapid decline into

Queen Elizabeth I, who believed in the supernatural and whose ghost now haunts Windsor Castle

melancholy and death. Perhaps not surprisingly her ghost, which haunts the Queen's Library at Windsor Castle, is said to be dressed all in black and to have a particularly wan face.

ENDOR WITCH

The story of King Saul and the apparition that the Witch of Endor raised from the bowels of the earth is perhaps the most famous ghost story in the Bible: a book that actually contains a number of references to phantoms and spirits. The account of the Endor Witch is found in Samuel 1: 28 and describes how King Saul, anxious at the possible outcome of his battle with the Philistines, summoned the old witch to raise the ghost of his predecessor, Samuel, for his advice. The spirit was apparently of little practical help and theologians have argued that the whole event was a fraud, the woman producing the spirit with smoke and its voice by ventriloquism. Nonetheless, the story has remained a famous one in the ghost lore to this day, discussed in innumerable studies of both the supernatural and witchcraft.

EVEREST GHOST

Everest, the world's highest mountain, is said to be haunted by the ghost of a climber who died on one of its treacherous slopes, and whose mission is now

The Witch of Endor raising a spirit before King Saul—an engraving by Schnorr von Carolsfeld

to encourage struggling mountaineers. In September 1975 it was revealed that Dougal Haston and Doug Scott had been aware of a "comforting presence" by their sides as they endured a very difficult night on the southwest face of Everest just under the 29,002-foot summit. This "ghostly third man" shared their snow-hole bivouac and encouraged them during the final hours before they made their successful last climb to the top. A theory has been advanced that the ghost is that of Andrew Irvine, who disappeared on Everest in 1924.

EXORCISM

The word exorcism has become commonplace and much abused in recent years primarily as a result of William Peter Blatty's best-selling novel, *The Exorcist* (1971), later made into an even more successful film. The act of exorcism is a religious ceremonial designed to remove spirits from either a possessed person or a haunted house. Christianity has a specific ritual to "drive out" any demons believed to be controlling a person's mind and this act is usually performed by a specially trained priest or clergyman. These men can also remove a troublesome ghost—such as a poltergeist—which is plaguing someone's home, and their ritual consists of prayer, loud exhortations, the sprinkling of holy water and the burning of either incense or candles. This is actually a modern version of the old church service of excommunication, where a sinner was barred from further worship by the priest who tolled a small bell, slammed shut the Bible after reading the malediction, and then extinguished the holy candles. This service has been referred to as "bell, book and candle." Although there have been numerous studies of exorcism and its powers, one of the most interesting and useful works is Father Herbert Thurston's *Ghosts and Poltergeists* (1953), which contains a special chapter, "The Exorcism of Haunted Houses" complete with full instructions and the litany for conducting a service of exorcism.

EXTRAS

An "extra" is a widely used term to describe faces that mysteriously appear on photographs of people who were either dead or not present at the time the picture was taken. This phenomenon occurred frequently during the early days of spirit photography and many of the faces were deliberately introduced onto the photographs by means of double exposure. Spirit mediums produced many such pictures, which were almost all fraudulent, but there have been other curious photographs taken over the years in which strange faces have appeared and where no fraud has been detected. Harry Price, the ghost-hunter and psychic investigator, collected a number of such photographs that still exist in the library he donated to the University of London. One of the most fascinating is the photograph on page 56 of an old man being menaced by a man with an axe. Although there is no doubt that it is a

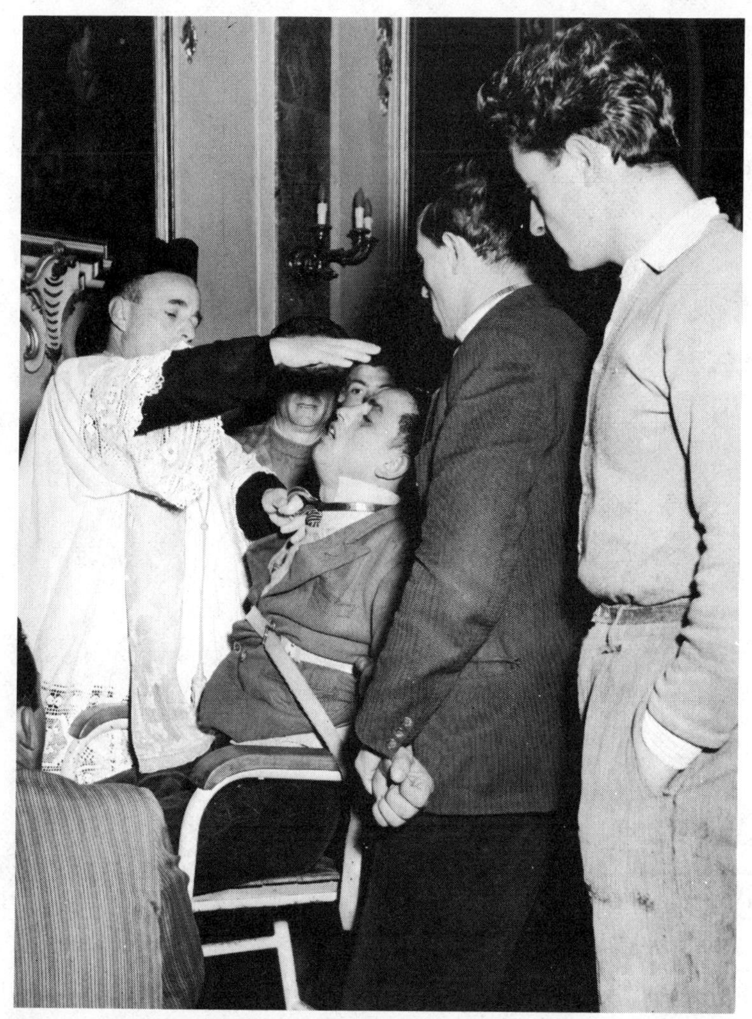

A priest conducting the service of exorcism on a man believed to be possessed by evil spirits

fake—created by double-exposing a glass negative—it is also a curious fact that the old man *did* die less than seven months after the photograph was taken as a result of a violent blow to the head! Harry Price discusses this whole phenomenon of "extras" in his book, *Search for Truth: My Life of Psychical Research* (1942).

ENFIELD POLTERGEIST

The ghostly disturbances that afflicted the Harper family in their two-story council house in Enfield, Middlesex, between 1977 and 1979 have become regarded as one of the most important and best-documented cases of a poltergeist in this century. The haunting consisted of strange noises, objects of furniture being moved about, and two young girls manhandled by invisi-

A spirit "extra" on a photograph which, though it is a fake, did prove to be an omen of the old man's death

ble hands that threw them from their beds. Other extraordinary phenomena followed—out-of-body trips were recorded by investigators, coins dropped from the ceilings, and teapots vanished from one room to appear in another. Guy Lyon Playfair, who reported the whole extraordinary story in *This House Is Haunted* (1980), along with his co-investigator, Maurice Grosse, witnessed some thirty incidents for which no normal explanation could be given, and includes in his book some remarkable photographs taken of the most baffling experiences undergone by the Harper family.

EPIC OF GILGAMESH

The *Epic of Gilgamesh* is an ancient Babylonian fable that may well be the earliest ghost story on record, dating from some 4,000 years ago. The Epic deals with the adventures of a great Babylonian hero called Gilgamesh who, having lost a close friend in battle, appeals to the god of the underworld, Negral, to restore him. After long entreating, Gilgamesh is suddenly surrounded by a great wind from which emerges a transparent human shape in the likeness of his friend. When the Babylonian is satisfied that the dead man is at peace he allows him to return to the "place of shades" and continues on his journey.

FAERY DOGS

The highlands and islands of Scotland are said to be the territory of spirits known as "faery dogs," which are green in color and about the size of two-year-old heifers. They have short tails and large feet, which leave sinister-looking footprints on the land or on the seashore. Usually they run silently in a very straight line, making no sound until they reach the place where they are to make their ominous bark. In a chapter on "The Fairy Dog" in his study, *The Ghost Book* (1955), Alasdair Alpin MacGregor says of this sound, "The bark of this terrifying quadruped is loud and clamorous. They say in the Isles that it barks but thrice. Since there is a fair interval of time between each bark, the human being, terror-stricken at hearing it, is often afforded an opportunity of reaching safety before the final and fatal bark is heard." The most persistent stories of faery dogs are to be found on the Isle of Tiree and there is even a cavern known traditionally as "the lair of the faery dog" where the barking of a huge dog can apparently be heard.

FETCH

The fetch, or co-walker, is a ghost-like vision of oneself, and to see one is generally believed to be an omen of death. John Aubrey, the folklorist, in his *Miscellanies* (1696) describes the appearance of several fetches.

> The beautiful Lady Diana Rich, daughter of the Earl of Holland, as she was walking in her father's garden at Kensington, to take the fresh air before dinner, about eleven o'clock, being then very well, met with her own apparition, habit, and every thing, as in a looking-glass. About a month after, she died of the small-pox. And it is said that her sister, the Lady Isabella Thynne, saw the like of herself also, before she died. This account I had from a person of honour.

Aubrey also recalls that the antiquarian Elias Ashmole told him that a certain Sir William Napier was warned in the same dreadful way while staying at an inn. On being shown to his room, he was horrified to see a corpse lying on the bed—and when he got closer he saw the figure exactly resembled himself! Although Sir William was a doctor and not given to superstitions, he died within a matter of days of reaching the end of his journey.

FILM GHOSTS

The ghost has been a popular feature in films since the very advent of silent movies—the ability of the camera to double-expose pictures and fade charac-

A quaint seventeenth-century picture of a woman being confronted by her fetch, or co-walker, a ghostly replica of herself

ters on and off the screen is ideally suited to producing realistic-looking spirits and phantoms. The great French pioneer filmmaker George Melies used all his earlier-won skill as a stage magician to introduce supernatural effects into his brilliant silent movies like *The Haunted Cave* (1898) and *The*

Devil's Manor (1900). It was not until 1922 that the first undeniable masterpiece with a ghostly theme reached the cinema—*The Conquering Power* made by the stylish American director Rex Ingram. The sequences featuring the ghost that ultimately brings about the death of the miser (a still is reproduced here) were both authentic and chilling. In 1936 the handsome British actor Robert Donat made a considerable impact as the long-dead Scotsman who accompanies his old home when it is transported to America in *The Ghost Goes West* and it is perhaps fair to say that this picture remains to this day the most famous "ghost film." A number of critics consider *The Uninvited* (1944) arguably the best of all such pictures, and certainly its atmospheric build-up of the story of a haunted house in Cornwall and the efforts of its occupants to banish the evil spirit are strikingly memorable. Ray Milland and Ruth Hussey as the brother and sister at the center of the story are outstanding, as is the beautiful Gail Russell, whose mediumistic powers help in the exorcism. Of all the ghost films produced in the intervening years, *The Innocents*, made in 1961, is perhaps the best remembered, though it fails to be as frightening as it should be. Based on Henry James's classic novel, *The Turn of the Screw* (1897), the picture is stylish but tends to explain the supernatural elements rather than leave them in the dark for the viewer to fathom out for himself, as James did. Further information on ghosts in films can be found in *An Illustrated History of the Horror Film* by Carlos Clarens (1967).

FIREBALL

The phenomenon known as a "fireball" is perhaps the strangest kind of phantom light, and in Scotland, where it has been widely reported, it is

A ghost haunting an old miser in the atmospheric film about the supernatural, *The Conquering Power*, made in 1922

known as the *gaelghan.* The ball resembles a globe of light and usually travels very smoothly and at a regular speed across stretches of water. Several accounts of these balls of fire have been collected by Alasdair Alpin MacGregor for his *The Ghost Book* (1955) in which he writes,

> People dwelling by Loch Rannoch-side, for example, have told me of the strange light in the form of a ball which at times skims a particular stretch of the loch's surface. Breadalbain's best known Ghost Lights are perhaps the two reputed to have been seen simultaneously on Loch Tay some years ago. And an old man whom I met in this locality about 1935 was one of many who declared that on the night before the interment of the bodies of two local young soldiers who were being brought home for burial, they had seen two bright balls of fire speeding along the surface of Loch Tay, on a course which the next day the boat carrying the coffins actually followed.

Fireballs are also mentioned in John Aubrey's *Miscellanies* (1696) and the whole phenomenon is discussed in *The Elements Rage* by Frank Lane (1945).

FIRE SPOOK OF CALEDONIA MILLS

Described as "the most weird, creepy and spooky mystery ever experienced in Canada," the mysterious fires that broke out in 1922 at a farmhouse in Caledonia Mills in Nova Scotia have puzzled psychic investigators ever since. The events in the house of Alexander Macdonald began a year earlier in 1921 when inexplicable tricks were played on him; these were quickly followed by fires that apparently ignited and burnt themselves out in small areas of the building during the night hours. Items of furnishing also mysteriously caught fire and strange lights glowed on and off in the house. In terror, Macdonald and his family of four fled from the "fire spook," as they named the phenomenon. Investigators who came to Caledonia Mills also saw the spontaneous outbreaks of fire and heard strange, pounding noises inside the farmhouse. They declared that "neither the fire nor the other strange happenings were the work of human hands." Although later enquiries were to accuse Macdonald's young daughter of being responsible for the "fire spook," the mystery has never been really satisfactorily solved, as R. S. Lambert says in his account of the story in *Exploring the Supernatural* (1955).

FLAMMARION, CAMILLE (1842–1925)

Flammarion, a French astronomer and writer, was one of the first popularizers of science and wrote several novels of fantasy, based on his interest in astronomy, which have been acclaimed as pioneer works of science fiction. Apart from worlds in space, Flammarion was deeply interested in the possibility of life after death and wrote several works on this theme including *The Inhabitants of the Other World* (1862) which consists of a series of revelations allegedly passed on to him by a medium named Mlle. Huet. Ghost stories also fascinated him and he personally investigated many cases of hauntings in

France. In 1890 he published *Haunted Houses*, in which he declared that he knew 180 houses that he was quite satisfied were haunted. He also quoted Cesare Lombroso (1836–1909), the Italian founder of the science of criminology, as his authority for a statement that there were 150 houses in England that were at that time tenantless because of mysterious sights and sounds.

FLYING DUTCHMAN

The legend of the phantom ship, the *Flying Dutchman*, is one of the most famous tales of the sea as well as being renowned in the annals of the supernatural. For centuries this doomed ship has sailed the oceans around the Cape of Good Hope bringing misfortune to any vessel unfortunate enough to cross her path. According to the legend, the *Dutchman* was captained by a man named Hendrik Vanderdecken who was returning home to Amsterdam by way of the Cape in the year 1641. A terrible storm had blown up, but Vanderdecken would not wait for it to die down, but cursed God and the elements saying that he would sail until Doomsday rather than stop. For his blasphemy—says the story—he was forced to sail on without ever being able to reach harbor, unless he could find another captain prepared to take a letter from him begging forgiveness. But over the years it has proved that any sailor who comes into contact with the *Dutchman* is doomed. History is replete with stories of seamen who have seen the terrible ship and indeed the legend has been immortalized in the opera, *Der Fliegende Holländer* (1843) by Richard Wagner, and Captain Frederick Marryat's marvelous sea yarn, *The Phantom Ship* (1839). The most famous sighting of the ship occurred in July 1881, when the eyewitness was Prince George (later King George V), who saw it while on board H.M.S. *Bacchante* on a world cruise. The Prince himself made the entry in the ship's log describing the encounter:

> July 11 1881. During the middle watch the so-called "Flying Dutchman" crossed our bows. She first appeared as a strange red light, as of a ship all aglow, in the midst of which light her masts, spars and sails, seemingly those of a normal brig, some two hundred yards distant from us, stood out in strong relief as she came up. Our lookout man on the forecastle reported her as close to our port bow, where also the officer of the watch from the bridge clearly saw her, as did our quarter-deck midshipman, who was sent forward at once to the forecastle to report back. But on reaching there, no vestige nor any sign of any material ship was to be seen either near or away to the horizon.

There was a tragic sequel to this report which once again fulfilled the prophecy of doom that surrounded the *Dutchman*. Prince George chronicles the facts: "During the forenoon watch the seaman who had this morning first reported this phantom vessel fell from our fore-topmast crosstrees and was killed instantly." And as if this was not bizarre enough, when the *Bacchante* reached port, its commander was struck down with a fatal illness. The most recent sighting of the *Flying Dutchman* was in October 1959 when—appropriately—a Captain P. Algra, master of the Dutch freighter, *Straat Magelhaen*, reported sighting her. "There was a queer rushing sound," he

A dramatic picture by Andre Castaigne of the most famous phantom of the seas, the *Flying Dutchman*

said, "then we saw a huge windjammer coming straight towards us. Her sails were fully spread, and we could clearly see a man at the wheel. So suddenly and so swiftly did she appear that there was no chance of turning aside, but just as she was due to strike the ship, she vanished into the darkness."

FOG-BOW

The fog-bow is a strange apparition reported for centuries by travellers in the Alps. Edward Whymper, who climbed the Matterhorn, described it thus in 1933: "A mighty arch appears high in the sky when the sun is behind the traveller's back. The arch gradually becomes a circle or an ellipse with a line down the middle, and then two faint crosses appear on either side. At the time of such an apparition there is a mist or fog, and the apparition is thrown upon the bank of fog." Not surprisingly, the fog-bow was believed for

The strange phenomenon of the fog-bow, which has intrigued many climbers in the Swiss Alps

generations to be a ghostly message of some kind, but it is now evident that it is caused by the refraction and reflection of light in much the same way as the more famous Specter of the Brocken in the Harz Mountains of Germany.

"FORTUNE HUNTER, THE"

One of the most famous ghost stories in South Africa, "The Fortune Hunter," concerns the former residence of General J. C. Smuts at Irene in the Transvaal. The Smuts family first encountered the ghost shortly after the Boer War. Their home had been built on the site of an old farmstead where a wealthy Boer farmer had lived prior to the approach of the British forces. When these soldiers appeared, he buried over £30,000 on the farm and disappeared. Later, during their occupancy of the site, the Smuts family several times saw an elderly gentleman, rather resembling President Kruger, searching the house and grounds. They were left in no doubt it was the ghost of the wealthy farmer returned to try and find his buried fortune.

FOSSEGRIM

The fossegrim, sometimes known as the "neck," is a river spirit who takes the form of a ghostly youth sitting in the middle of a stream playing a harp. He is said to be harmless, although he can be cruel to young girls who are fickle with their affections, according to old European traditions. In some parts of the continent it is believed to be a good idea to carry an unsheathed knife whenever you are out in a boat on a river as this will "bind the neck." There is a certain similarity between the fossegrim and the Scottish kelpie.

FOUNDATION STONE

There is ghost lore at the root of the ancient tradition of ceremonially laying the first stone of a new building. The ancient pagans such as the Vikings and the Saxons believed that each house needed its own spirit to defend it against the attentions of other malevolent spirits and consequently would make a sacrifice of a human victim by immuring him up alive in the walls of the construction. The ghost that resulted would then serve as a guardian of the place. It is a grim fact that in numerous instances it was a child that was selected as a victim, for the young were believed to make particularly wretched and frightening phantoms. The traditional phrase associated with old houses about there being "a skeleton in every cupboard" resulted from this practice.

FOUNTAIN OF BLOOD

A ghostly vision of a fountain of blood has been repeatedly witnessed in Battle Abbey, Sussex, England which William the Conqueror built on the spot where he triumphed over King Harold in 1066. The fountain is said to represent all the blood spilled during that terrible battle and on occasions it has been reported that the specter of King Harold, complete with an arrow in his eye, has also been seen in the vicinity.

FOX SISTERS

The Fox sisters, Margaret (1838–1893) and Kate (1841–1892) are claimed to have been the originators of spiritualism as an organized movement seeking to establish life after death. This followed their experiences during the last century at Hydesville in New York State. Their home was said to be haunted by a ghost that made strange rapping noises, and in 1848 the girls devised a means of apparently communicating with this spirit, whom they called "Mr. Splitfoot," by tapping out messages in code—different numbers of taps signifying specific questions and answers. As a result of information received from the ghost, digging took place in the cellar of the Fox home and a skeleton was found—seemingly verifying the spirit's sad story of its death and burial. Such was the sensation caused by this story that soon others were trying similar means of making contact with the dead—and spiritualism was born. The Fox sisters, however, led far from happy lives thereafter—at one time confessing that the events at Hydesville were all fraudulent and then almost immediately retracting this "confession." Nonetheless, they set in motion a movement now world-wide. There are numerous studies of the Fox sisters and spiritualism in general, of which *Spiritualism: Its History, Phe-*

The Fox Sisters, the American founders of spiritualism: Margaret (*left*) and Kate

nomena and Doctrine by J. A. Hill (1918) and *Spiritualism Today* by Maurice Barbanell (1969) can be recommended.

FREMANTLE MUSEUM, THREE GHOSTS OF

The stately Gothic building that serves as the Fremantle Maritime Museum in Western Australia can boast no fewer than three ghosts. This is not so surprising when the visitor realizes the building was originally erected by convicts in 1865, and was used as a lunatic asylum until 1909. Inmates were subjected to various brutal forms of "treatment" like the "hot box" and the padded cell, and it is believed that it is the spirits of three of them that now wander the building. Each ghost has its individual characteristics. One is a kindly soul who kisses and cuddles people, a second is aggressive and snatches things as well as rattling doors, while the third is an old woman who appears to be searching for something. According to the museum staff there have been many incidents with these three ghosts, although they add, "Nothing ever happens when the museum is full of visitors. Only when the place is quiet do we have these contacts."

G

GALLEY BEGGAR

The galley beggar is an extraordinary English ghost found mostly in the North of England and first mentioned in Reginald Scot's work, *The Discoverie of Witchcraft* (1584). It is a very thin spirit, often looking like a skeleton, and its main purpose seems to be to terrify anyone it encounters; indeed its name comes from "gally," meaning to frighten or scare. It also, apparently, has the ability to go headless if it so desires! The most famous galley beggar haunts a hill between Over and Nether Stowey in Somerset and it careers about on a toboggan with its head tucked under its arm shrieking with laughter! A relative of this spirit is the bull beggar, which appears in Surrey and can travel with enormous leaps.

GALLEYTROT

The galleytrot is an animal spirit resembling a huge dog, which is said to move about the country lanes of England "like an evil whisper." According

A turn-of-the century photographer's idea of the strange skeleton-like ghost known as the galley beggar

to Alasdair Alpin MacGregor in his *The Ghost Book* (1955) galleytrot is thought to be a corruption of *gardez le trésor* or "guard the treasure," and indeed the animal is mostly to be found in the vicinity of old burial grounds or hidden treasure. He says that one of the most fearsome galleytrots lurks in the wilds of Suffolk and resembles an enormous hound with a monk's head! He adds, "The phantom is also known in Essex, particularly in those parts of the country bordering Suffolk. A black specimen is said to cross the county boundary when travelling between the villages of Middleton in Essex and Boxford in West Suffolk."

GHOST CLUB

According to Peter Underwood, who has been president of the London-based Ghost Club, it is the oldest organization associated with psychic matters,

The galleytrot, a ghost in the form of a huge dog, as pictured in *Tales of Terror* (1825)

having been originally founded in the early 1860s. Over the years the club has investigated psychic phenomena in all forms, and had among its members some distinguished and highly reputable men and women. The club meets regularly to discuss all matters pertaining to the paranormal and has a large collection of material on ghostly matters. Mr. Underwood is the author of several valuable books on ghosts, and will provide details of the club if contacted c/o The Savage Club, Fitzmaurice Place, Berkeley Square, London W1Z 6JD, England.

GHOST DANCE

The ghost dance is a famous ritual among many of the tribes of North American Indians and is a ceremony to pay respect to the dead and implore their spirits not to trouble the living. It is a noisy, colorful and exciting dance that is believed to please the ghosts, while at the same time demonstrating to them that the tribe has many braves who will attack the phantoms if they dare to intervene in the Indians' affairs. The Indians also believe that ghosts themselves are noisy beings and there is a saying among the tribes that "the shadow souls of the dead chirp like crickets."

GHOST FIGURES

Ghostly faces and figures appearing unexpectedly on photographs of natural formations such as groves of bushes and trees, among rock clusters, and even on cloud formations, have proved plentiful in recent years—and are invari-

The "ghost figure" of the Virgin Mary, which appeared in France in 1956 but that proved to be just a trick of the light

ably explainable as a trick of the light. One of the best known of these was the photograph reproduced here taken at Metz in France in 1956 and claimed to show the ghostly form of the Virgin Mary. It was, in fact, caused by the light shining through the trees. The subject is discussed in some detail in *Phenomena* by John Michell and Robert J. M. Rickard (1977).

GHOST-HUNTERS

There have been numerous important ghost-hunters this century, of whom the Englishman Harry Price and the American Hans Holzer are perhaps the best known. Over the years they have been able to call on the latest develop-

The ghost-hunter's kit belonging to researcher Harry Price, which he took with him whenever he investigated any haunting

ments in science and technology in their quest to establish beyond all reasonable doubt the authenticity of a haunting. Harry Price has given full details of how to become a ghost-hunter in his book *Fifty Years of Psychical Research* (1939), which included the photograph here of his ghost-hunter's kit, although more up-to-date techniques are now being operated by both the Institute of Psychophysical Research, Oxford, and the Society for Psychical Research based in London. The Ghost Club, also in London, has similarly encouraged the work of ghost-hunters in many varied locations.

GHOST STORIES

Ghost stories have been told since the earliest times, and they have become the traditional type of story to be spun around the fireside on cold winter evenings, particularly at Christmas time. The number of collections of ghost stories, either by one author or many writers, runs into thousands and they already fill the entire libraries of collectors. Ranging from the traditional ghost tales of folklore to the works of modern masters like M. R. James and Algernon Blackwood, the very best of them seek to present ghosts in a way that makes them believable to the reader however much of a skeptic he may be. There have been numerous studies of ghost stories and the following can be recommended to the general reader: *The Supernatural in Fiction* by Peter Penzoldt (1952), *The Supernatural in Modern English Fiction* by Dorothy Scarborough (1917) and *Night Visitors: The Rise and Fall of the English Ghost Story* by Julia Briggs (1977). Despite the enormous and continuing interest in ghost stories, there have been very few magazines concentrating on publishing such tales, although they do appear regularly in newspapers and other periodicals at appropriate times of the year. A rare exception to this rule was *Ghost Stories*, a well-read "pulp" magazine that appeared in the 1930s and contained "real-life" sightings as well as fictional tales of hauntings. Publisher Harold Hersey managed to combine both sensation and solid fact into a mix that made it popular for the few years it survived and subsequently

The pulp magazine, *Ghost Stories*, which appeared in the 1930s and is now much collected

a much sought-after collector's item. A magazine published earlier called *The Ghost* (*c.* 1836) had actually very little to do with the supernatural and was packed with tales of freaks, monsters, wild men, cruel customs, cannibalism and many other similar topics illustrated with crude woodcuts!

GHOST TRAIN

The ghost train, that popular feature of the fun-fair, has a "real life" equivalent. According to the *Morning Post* of November 14, 1928, the 1:20 P.M. train from Newton Abbot in Devon to Paddington, London was regarded as an unlucky train on account of the number of fatalities associated with it. Mr. J.

Hibber of Newton Abbot, who drove it to London, was taken ill when the train was travelling at express speed. He was removed to a waiting-room at Exeter Station, where he died a few minutes later. A few months previously, Fireman Powlessland had died as the train steamed into Paddington, and in November 1927 Fireman Walters had been killed while getting the engine ready for its run. Because of these three fatalities in less than twelve months, the train became known as "the ghost train." In this country, there is a famous legend concerning the funeral train that carried the coffin of President Abraham Lincoln to his last resting place in 1865. Almost every April since then, says the story, this same phantom train rolls along the same stretch of track in New York State—complete with a military band playing, although no human ears can hear it! There is also, of course, a famous stage play called *The Ghost Train* by John Alexander and Arnold Ridley, which has been delighting audiences for almost fifty years.

GHOSTS

Ghosts, as innumerable studies have shown, are world-wide phenomena, recorded throughout history, appearing in many different shapes and forms, and with a variety of purposes. The most widespread is, of course, the ghost of a human being—appearing as a mist-like entity, roughly human in shape, and disappearing as mysteriously and suddenly as it appeared. In this author's view, the best definition of a ghost has been provided by the poet and writer, Robert Graves (b. 1895) who wrote in an article "What I Believe About Ghosts" (1941):

> The commonsense view is, I think, that one should accept ghosts very much as one accepts fire—a more common but equally mysterious phenomenon. What is fire? It is not really an element, not a principle of motion, not a living creature—not even a disease, though a house can catch it from its neighbours. It is an event rather than a thing or a creature. Ghosts, similarly, seem to be events rather than things or creatures—and nearly always disagreeable events.

GHOSTS, TYPES

According to G. N. M. Tyrell in his book, *Apparitions* (1953), there are four main categories of ghosts. 1. Experimental ghosts, in which the spirits of people who are still alive are made to appear by them to others at different places. 2. Crisis ghosts, who appear to relatives when those to whom they belong are going through some terrible trial, most probably dying. 3. Postmortem ghosts—these appear long enough after a person's death so as not to be confused with crisis ghosts; they usually look and seem so like the real person that they leave viewers in a profound state of shock. 4. True ghosts are the most widely reported and are seen by people who have no connection with them whatsoever; they are not governed by time, appearing centuries after death, but usually restricted to one locality.

THE GHOST.

No. 5.] WEDNESDAY, FEB. 27. [*Price One Penny.*

THE DANCE OF THE DEAD.

MANY a century back, an aged wandering bagpiper settled at Neisse, a small town in Silesia. He lived quietly and honestly, and at first played his tunes in secret for his own amusement; but it was not long, as his neighbours delighted in listening to him, and would often in the calm of a warm midsummer evening gather round his door, whilst he called forth the cheering sounds of harmony, before Master Willibald became acquainted both with old and young, was flattered and caressed, and lived in content and prosperity.

The gallant beaux of the place, who had near his door first beheld those lovely creatures, for whose sake they had written so much bad poetry, and lost so much more valuable time, were his constant customers for melting songs, while they drowned the softer passages with the depth of their sighs. The old citizens invited him at their solemn dinner parties; and no bride would have deemed her wedding-feast to be completely celebrated, had not Master Willibald played the bridal-dance of his own composition. For this very purpose he had invented a most tender melody, which united gaiety and gravity, playful ideas and melancholy feelings, forming a true emblem of matrimonial life. A feeble trace of this tune is still to be found in what is called the old German "Grandfather's dance," which, as far down as the time of our parents, was an important requisite of a wedding-feast, and is even heard now and then in our days. As often as Master Willibald played this tune, the prudest spinster would not refuse to dance, the stooping matron moved again her time-stiffened joints, and the grey-haired grandfather danced it merrily with the

One of the earliest ghost-story magazines, *The Ghost* published about 1836. It actually carried very little about spirits!

GHOULS

The ghoul is an Arabian ghost that appears in human form with a hideous face and makes a specialty of stealing corpses. It usually haunts any area used for the burial of the dead, and its favorite trick is carrying off the bodies of children. Over the centuries it has been reported throughout the whole of the Muslim world from India to Africa, and its demonic activities have made it much feared. It is often compared with other vampire-like creatures, but unlike them has no substance and anything that comes into contact with it passes straight through. Despite this, it is believed to feed on human bodies, and there are many stories of ghouls that have preyed on travellers unlucky enought to fall ill while crossing the desert. See further details in *The Realm of Ghosts* by Eric Maple (1964).

GIANT GHOST OF STAWELL

Australia can claim what is believed to be the only ghost of a giant—a huge phantom over eight feet high that haunts an old house at Stawell, a mining town about 145 miles from Melbourne. So terrifying is this ghost that during the past decade it has driven ten families from the premises. All the families, including adults and children, have reported seeing the apparition in either the front yard or the kitchen. Although the house has long had an evil reputation in the district, no theories have yet been advanced as to the origin of this extraordinary giant ghost!

GLAD WISH WOOD

Rudyard Kipling's famous story *Puck of Pook's Hill* (1906) was partly inspired by a ghost "full of a sense of ancient ferocity and evil" that haunted Glad Wish Wood, close to his home, Bateman's in Burwash, Sussex. Kipling (1865–1936) was fascinated by what he called "haunted landscapes"; and Pook's Hill, to the rear of Bateman's, was even more directly responsible for his famous book. It is dotted with prehistoric dwellings and earthworks seemingly alive with the spirits of the past. At Kipling's prompting, a ghost hunt was held in Glad Wish Wood and one of the members reported seeing a shape that "coughed, choked and moaned as it walked . . . and its fingers were also plucking at its throat." Later research revealed that a man named David Leany had been hanged for murder in the woods in 1728, but had protested his innocence and vowed to return and haunt those who had put him to death. Kipling, of course, wrote about ghosts in several of his short stories, in particular "The Phantom Rickshaw" (1895), "My Own True Ghost Story" (1895) and "The House Surgeon" (1909), as well as in other fine tales to be found in the collections of his works.

GLAMIS CASTLE

Thirteenth-century Glamis Castle in Angus is probably Britain's most famous haunted building, and there is certainly no more archetypal ghost locality than this gray stone castle with its mist-shrouded turrets and dark battlements. The castle is famous for its association with Shakespeare's play *Macbeth* (although there is no evidence that King Duncan stayed here or was even murdered in the building), the half-man, half-beast monster that is supposed to lurk somewhere among the uncounted rooms (and may have been a deformed son of one of the previous Earls of Strathmore who lived here) and the phantom known as "the gray lady," who haunts the small family chapel and is believed to be Lady Glamis, wife of the sixth Lord Glamis, who was convicted of witchcraft in 1540 and burned alive at the stake. The castle is also renowned as the seat of the the Bowes-Lyons family, and the present Queen Mother was born there as well as giving birth to Princess Margaret in the same room. In recent years a poltergeist has also been reported at Glamis, disturbing the slumber of anyone who sleeps in a particular room. The story of this fascinating castle and its history has been told in many books, in particular Lord Halifax's *Ghost Book* published in 1936 and much reprinted.

The famous Gray Lady who haunts the magnificent Glamis Castle in Scotland

GLANVILL, JOSEPH (1636–80)

Joseph Glanvill has been called "the father of modern psychical research" and his book *Sadducimus Triumphatus* (1666), which investigated "the full and plain evidence concerning witches and apparitions," is an important pioneer work into the supernatural. A deeply learned and intelligent man, Glanvill was the first writer to bring skepticism and objectivity to bear on a variety of stories concerning witchcraft and ghosts. His interest had been fired by personal involvement in the case of the Drummer of Tedworth, as well as his firmly held conviction that science could explain the supernatural. His research was painstaking, and apart from attending witch trials and meeting people who claimed to have seen ghosts, he was also present at a number of seances and cross-examined the mediums concerned. Although there is no doubt that Glanvill was duped by a number of people, and parts of his *Sadducismus Triumphatus* are undoubtedly naive in their conclusions, he did instigate many of the methods of psychical research that are still widely practiced today. As Harry Price wrote in his book, *Poltergeist Over England* (1945): "He it was who first stimulated those persons fortunate enough to possess a ghost, to investigate the affair in a proper manner, to record the case systematically, and to have the phenomenon attested by responsible witnesses."

GRAVE SLEEPERS

The Celtic people had a strange ritual for contacting the ghosts of their forebears known as "grave sleeping." During it, men believed to be suitably receptive would sleep on the graves of their ancestors, and if the spirits had messages to communicate they would enter the bodies of the sleepers and drive them into wild fits. While possessed, the men would shake and scream out the messages from "the other side."

GRAVEYARD

An old English tradition says that the ghost of the first person buried in any graveyard is responsible for guarding it against the Devil, and therefore has special powers. Sometimes a completely black dog would be buried in the new graveyard before any human being so that it could take on this onerous task. These ghostly guardians of the dead were known as "church grims."

GREEN LADIES

Green ladies are without doubt more numerous in Scotland than anywhere else, according to Francis Watt and the Reverend Andrew Carter in their *Picturesque Scotland* (1929). They quote the three best-known examples as the Green Lady of the Carnegies; a grayish-green phantom who haunted the family of a former laird of Newton; and the green lady who always appeared to herald a death in the Burnett family of Crathes. Another green lady, also known as the Siannag or Elle maid, is said to have haunted the Campbell family when they lived at ancient Dunstaffnage Castle on Loch Etive.

GREMLIN

Gremlins are the most recent type of apparition to be reported—for although the word is now widely used, it actually originated as recently as the Second World War. Simply stated, the gremlin is a spirit accused of vexing airmen, and the first reports of them came from pilots flying dangerous wartime missions who were suddenly conscious of seeing misty, goblin-like figures lurking in their aircraft. It was the pilots themselves who nicknamed them "gremlins" and it became generally assumed, as they did little more than play the occasional pranks on aircrews, that their purpose was more friendly than antagonistic. Ghost-hunter Alasdair Alpin MacGregor mentions them in his work, *The Ghost Book* (1955), writing: "Members of the Royal Air Force, who participated in the Battle of Britain, have told me of them; and, although the *Oxford English Dictionary* fails to include the word, a professor at Oxford tells his friend, the eminent A. L. Rowse, that the gremlins 'have been at me all my life.'" Recently there have been stories of gremlins making their presence felt in large factories, and from this the suggestion has emerged that they may be entities somehow formed by the working of machines.

GRAY LADIES

Stories of ghosts described as "ladies in gray" almost all originate from the Tudor period when the wholesale destruction of abbeys and monasteries resulted in the death of many nuns who were then habited in gray. There are famous gray ladies to be found at Newstead Abbey, Rufford Abbey, as well as Holy Trinity Church in Micklegate, York.

GRAY MAN

The gray man or *Bodach Glas* to whom Sir Walter Scott refers in his novel *Waverley* (1814) was a real phantom that appeared to the Eglinton family. It appeared to the Earl of Eglinton, who died in 1861, no less than three times—the final occasion being on the golf course at St. Andrews! According to the legend, the Earl suddenly stopped in mid-stroke and said to his companion, "I can play no longer, there is the *Bodach Glas*. I have seen it for the third time, something fearful is going to happen to me." That very night he died.

GRISLY GHOST OF GUY

The story of the Grisly Ghost of Guy is one of the earliest and best documented in Europe, and concerns a spirit voice that was heard in the year 1323 in the home of a Frenchman who had recently died. The setting was the town of Alais in Provence, and the voice was said to belong to a certain Guy de Torno. So great was the alarm caused by the unearthly sounds that a group of four friars from the local priory were asked to investigate and according to existing accounts, actually held a conversation with the ghost. The friars went about their enquiry in a very scientific manner, and seemed to rule out all possibility of fraud, declaring themselves convinced at the end of eight days that the home of Guy de Torno was indeed haunted by the spirit of its former occupant. The spirit apparently told the friars that the only way he could be released from haunting the building was if they would say one hundred Masses for his soul. After this was done, the Grisly Ghost of Guy was heard no more. Subsequent investigation has pointed to the fact that the haunting may have been the work of Guy's widow who was said to be a somewhat hysterical person and might have manufactured the voice by ventriloquism. Nonetheless the case remains a famous one, recorded in several old manuscripts and a long Middle English poem. It is also discussed in detail in *Ghosts and Poltergeists* by Herbert Thurston (1953).

GUS THE NAZI

"Gus the Nazi" was the name given to an extraordinary poltergeist first reported in Bavaria in 1949. According to local accounts, the invisible spirit took exception to German women who fraternized with the Allied Occupation troops and terrified several of them by throwing objects at them or tipping them out of bed. On one notable occasion he has said to have cropped the hair of a girl in full view of her parents! Douglas Hill tells the story of Gus the Nazi in *Man, Myth & Magic* (No. 39, 1970).

HAG OF THE DRIBBLE

The Hag of the Dribble is the popular name for the evil-looking Welsh ghost called the gwrach-y-rhibyn. The spirit takes the form of a dreadful old hag with long, matted hair, a hooked nose, piercing eyes, a crooked back and long arms with claw-like fingers. These arms are sometimes described as looking

The Hag of the Dribble, one of the best-known and most-feared Welsh ghosts

rather like scaly black wings. She has a high-pitched voice that is said to be an omen of death when heard. According to tradition she only haunts old Welsh families—a characteristic of the Irish banshee—and among these can be numbered the Stradlings of St. Donat's Castle, near Llantwit, the De Clares of Caerphilly Castle, near Cardiff, and the Barrys of South Wales. Perhaps the most famous site haunted by a gwrach-y-rhibyn is the ruins of Pennard Castle. The origin of the hag is unknown, according to John Rhys in his study, *Celtic Folk Lore* (1901), although she may be the spirit of one of the ancient Welsh goddesses. Wirt Sykes in his book, *British Goblins* (1880), maintains that sometimes the cry of the hag is intelligible. When it is a man that is going to die, she cries, "Oh, oh! fy ngwr fy ngwr!" (my husband, my husband) and when a child is doomed, "Fy mlentyn, fy mlentyn bach" (my child, my little child). He also notes that "She is as ugly as the *Gwrach-y-rhibyn!*" used to be a saying in Wales.

HAIRY HANDS GHOST

One of the most extraordinary hauntings in Britain occurs on Dartmoor near the village of Postbridge. There have been several reports of travellers and drivers suddenly being seized by a disembodied pair of hairy hands that wrestle them to the ground, or any vehicle they may be driving off the road. The legend is discussed in detail in *Legends of Devon* by J. R. W. Coxhead.

HALLOWEEN

The night of Halloween, October 31, is supposed by tradition to be the best time of the year for actually seeing ghosts. On this one night they are said to be able to appear and mingle with the other denizens of the dark such as witches and warlocks. It is traditional on Halloween to wear fancy dress and make pumpkin heads with lighted candles, and for children to go out dressed in ghostly costumes and knock at people's doors demanding, "Trick or treat?" Only by being rewarded with a sweet is the child prevented from playing a prank. In actual fact the significance of the night is far more sinister than this, for Halloween was originally a festival of the powers of darkness when great fires were lit across the countryside to summon the spirits of the dead and placate them by giving them warmth to see them through the cold of the coming winter. It originated long before the advent of Christianity and also marked the passage of summer into winter. Though in England the bonfire tradition has been transferred to November 5 to mark the arrest of Guy Fawkes—purely an action by the Church to disguise the pagan origins of the festival—the belief that ghostly things occur on Halloween still persists.

HALLUCINATIONS, CENSUS OF

One of the first surveys to find out how many people believed they had seen a ghost was conducted in 1889 by the Society for Psychical Research. The society asked a single question of the 17,000 people they contacted: "Have you

Playing pranks on Halloween—a delightful magic lantern slide

ever, when believing yourself to be completely awake, had a vivid impression of seeing or being touched by a living being or inanimate object, or of hearing a voice; which impression, so far as you could discover, was not due to any external physical cause?" From the cross-section of the public to whom the census was directed, 15,316 replied they had not, while 1,684 thought they had. From these figures, the society reported, it seemed that only 10 per cent of human beings had had such a supernatural experience, and of this 10 per cent, 66 per cent said that it had only occurred once in their lives.

HAMMERSMITH GHOST

Still well remembered is the story of the Hammersmith Ghost, which caused something of a sensation in the winter of 1804. People in the district became alarmed by tales of a very tall, white figure that arose from a local churchyard and attempted to accost passers-by. One woman to whom the ghost appeared died of fright as the result of her experience, and both men and women began to avoid going out in the neighborhood at night. The suggestion was advanced by certain people that the ghost belonged to a young man who had committed suicide by cutting his throat so his spirit could not rest. Others felt the figure might be more flesh and blood, and a group of stout-nerved citizens set up a vigilante committee to try and catch the phantom. For three nights they lay in wait and nothing happened. And then on the fourth night, a white figure suddenly hove out of the darkness. A shot rang out and the figure dropped. When the vigilantes rushed forward they found the "ghost" was indeed a man—an unfortunate bricklayer named Thomas Milwood who had been returning home late from work and was still wearing his cement-stained overalls! Despite such a prosaic ending, the story caught the imagination of pamphlet writers and ballad singers and became widely known. There were still those, however, who felt a real ghost lurked in Hammersmith, and one pamphleteer concluded his account, "The ghost was never discovered and is still living." The story has also been immortalized in numerous illustrations, including the one shown on page 82 made in 1804.

HAMPTON COURT PALACE

The magnificent palace of Hampton Court beside the River Thames in England has been a favorite with visitors and tourists for many years, and has the added attraction of one of the best attested ghost stories. The phantom is said to be that of Mistress Sibell Penn, who was foster-mother to Edward VI after the sudden death of his mother, Jane Seymour, in 1537. The old lady lived in rooms in the south-west wing of the palace and remained totally devoted to the young king until her death from smallpox in 1562. As a reward she was buried in Hampton Church beneath a handsome monument complete with full-length effigy, and there she lay in peace until the church was pulled down in 1829. During the demolition, Mistress Penn's grave was

A contemporary engraving of the Hammersmith Ghost, which created such a sensation in 1804—and had such a simple explanation!

evidently disturbed, and soon thereafter her ghostly form began to haunt the palace. She was instantly recognizable in her long, straight dress and tight-fitting cap from the likeness on her monument. In the one hundred and fifty years since, the restless shade of the old nurse has continued to be seen and heard in the palace, and makes a visit to the south-west wing of Hampton Court a must for every ghost-hunter. There are claims that two other ghosts haunt the palace—Queen Katherine Howard, whose screams of terror have been heard in the Haunted Gallery, and Jane Seymour herself, who is supposed to appear in the Queen's Rooms dressed all in white and carrying a lighted candle.

HARPY

The harpy is a ghost-like creature with the wings of a bird and the face of a woman, which was believed by the ancient Greeks to be a wind spirit that could interfere in the affairs of man if not regularly propitiated. This "bad wind" blew particularly against ships at sea and during harvest time, and would occasionally seek after the actual souls of men and women. In order to please the harpy, the Greeks made sacrifices of sheep to her at regular intervals during the year.

HAUNTED CHAIRS

Old chairs still occupied by the ghosts of a former owner are a not infrequent occurrence in supernatural lore. The best known such story is that related by the authoress Maria Edgeworth (1767–1849), who wrote the Gothic masterpiece *Castle Rackrent* (1800). She describes having seen a ghostly shape occupying a chair at her home in Edgeworthstown while she and her father were awaiting the arrival of a cousin who often stayed with them. The apparition gradually took on the shape of this expected relative and then dramatically announced that the ship in which he was returning had been shipwrecked and he was the sole survivor. At this the figure disappeared, and although Maria was still shaken by the experience she was glad to hear that her cousin was apparently safe. In fact, it later transpired that while the ship had indeed foundered at the time the ghost materialized in the chair, it was the cousin who had been the only person on board to perish! Ghost-hunter Alasdair MacGregor has devoted a chapter to "Haunted Chairs" in his book *Phantom Footsteps* (1959) and discusses the strange case of the photograph of a ghost in a chair taken about 1910 by Mr. Sherard Cowper-Coles at Rossal House, Sunbury-on-Thames. The house was itself believed to be haunted by the ghost of an old lady and the photograph—reproduced over and not yet proved a fake—seemed to substantiate the claim.

HAUNTED CHESTS

There are numerous accounts of haunted chests to be found among the classic studies of ghost lore, perhaps the most famous story appearing in Joseph Glanvill's *Sadducismus Triumphatus* (1683). This is the case of the Iron

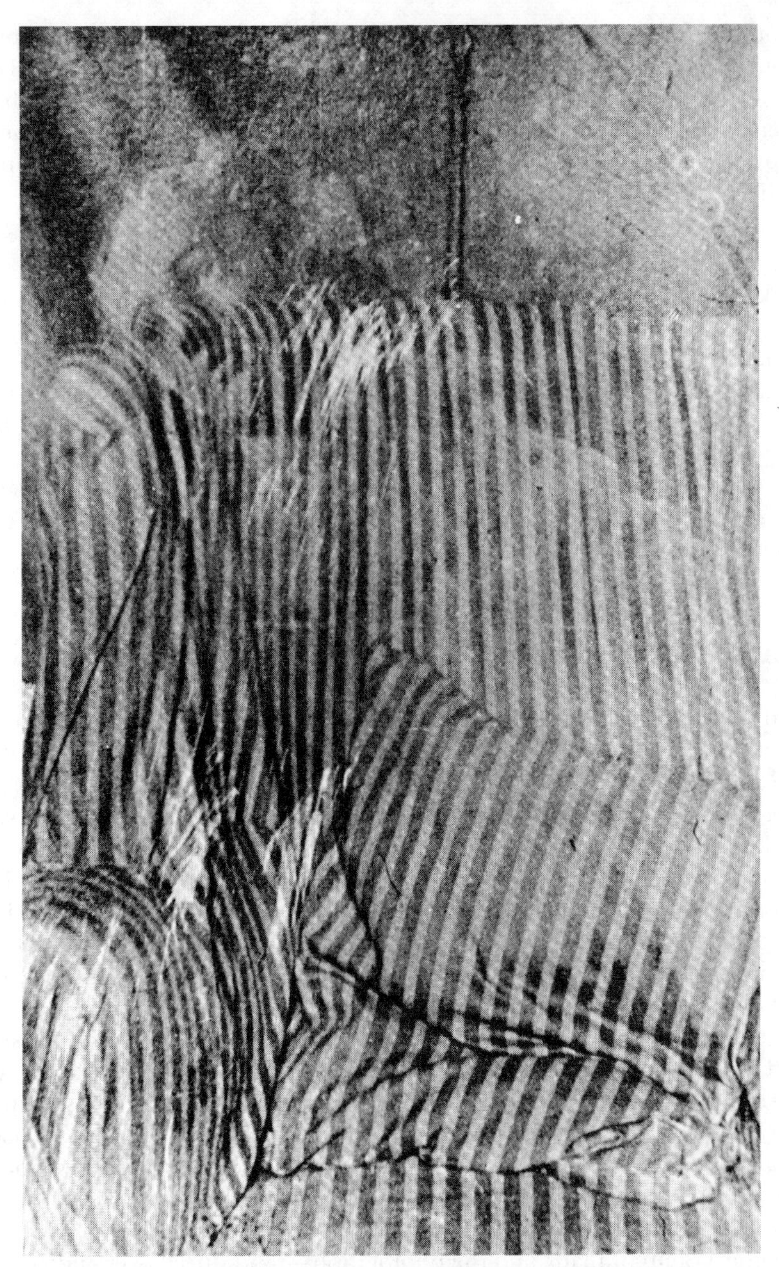

The haunted chair at Sunbury-on-Thames, England, investigated by ghost-hunter Alasdair Alpin MacGregor

Chest of Durley in which the death of a Mr. John Bourne of Durley in Somerset was prophesied by the opening and shutting of an iron chest that stood in his bedroom. The events occurred in the year 1654 while Mr. Bourne was lying ill in bed. Both he, his doctor and his sister-in-law, who were present at the time, saw the three locks of the chest click open, then the lid slowly rise up. Seeing a misty shape appear, Mr. Bourne cried out, "I'll be with you, by and by" and fell back never to regain consciousness. In his interesting book, *Gazetteer of British Ghosts* (1971), Peter Underwood recounts the story of the poltergeist chest that stood in Stanbury Manor, Morwenstow in Cornwall and was believed to have been brought to England with the Spanish Armada. The chest was covered with hideous, carved figures, and earned its reputation because of the strange events that happened around it. Underwood offers an interesting suggestion that the disturbances might have been caused because of a story that the body of a man with his throat cut had once been found in it!

HAUNTED WARDROBE

The following advertisement appeared in the *Morning Post* of August 19, 1937: "Haunted Wardrobe—Advertiser will be glad to deliver same to anybody interested, complete with ghost, which would also, no doubt, feel more at home if welcomed."

The owner was a lady living in Carterton, Oxfordshire, who said that the cupboards and drawers of the wardrobe frequently opened and closed of their own accord, and the phantom figure of a man had been seen in the same room that the piece of furniture occupied. Once the wardrobe changed hands, however, the haunting inexplicably ceased.

HAUNTING

The word haunting is used to describe the appearance on a number of occasions of a ghostly figure that appears of its own volition. Any specific building or locality where such a manifestation occurs is referred to as being haunted, and there are innumerable accounts of such places all over the world. Although there has been intensive investigation into hauntings for many years, it is quite impossible to collect any figures as to just how many haunted places exist, although a survey in the United States gave some indication as to how widespread was the belief in ghosts. The result of this survey, published in October 1979, reported surprisingly that only 21 per cent of children believed in ghosts—but over 57 per cent of adults were convinced of their existence!

HAWTHORNE, NATHANIEL (1804–64)

Born in the witch-haunted New England town of Salem, Nathaniel Hawthorne utilized the supernatural a great deal in his work, and apart from well-known novels like the famous *House of the Seven Gables* (1851), several of his short stories must be among the most anthologized in the whole macabre genre—"The White Old Maid" and "Young Goodman Brown" being two notable examples. Hawthorne actually saw a ghost himself in 1840 while he was living in Boston and retold the strange experience in "The

An eighteenth-century engraving of a haunted chest believed to be of an American haunting

Ghost of Doctor Harris," which was not actually published until some years after his death in the *Nineteenth Century* magazine of January 1900. The story concerns an aged clergyman whom Hawthorne saw several times reading a newspaper in his customary spot in the Athenaeum Club *weeks after his death!* For a man so steeped in the supernatural, it is perhaps not surprising to learn that Hawthorne himself returned as a ghost, presenting himself to his son, Julian (1846–1934) on one notable occasion! Julian Hawthorne himself wrote several stories about the supernatural including, "The Spectre of the Camera" (1915).

HEADLESS GHOSTS

There are quite a number of legends in existence of ghosts being seen headless, or else carrying their heads underneath their arms! Such phantoms are almost invariably people who were beheaded, and perhaps the most famous member of their ranks is Anne Boleyn, one of Henry VIII's wives. She was executed in the Tower of London, and for centuries her splendidly dressed figure with head tucked under her right arm was said to walk through the precincts of the tower on cold, dark nights. Perhaps surprisingly, she has also been seen with her head in its correct place! In Scotland, the headless ghost of a clan chief named Ewen Maclaine haunts his family home in Mull, although he died of a sword thrust in battle; while in this country the ghost of Nellie Macquillie wanders headless through a small town in North Carolina though she actually died peacefully in bed! The two best-known stories of headless ghosts are certainly those of Lord Lovat and St. Denis. Simon Lovat (*c.* 1667–1747) was a Scottish chief whose wild and lawless life and frequent plotting against the monarchy ended in his trial and execution by beheading in London in 1747. Thereafter his ghost was often seen at night, pacing about the house tops, and carrying its head underneath its arm. William Hogarth, who had sketched Lovat during his trial, also painted a picture of him entitled *Lovat's Ghost on Pilgrimage* of which George III declared that it "thrilled him with terror." St. Denis, the apostle of France and first Bishop of Paris, was certainly a more illustrious ghost, and after his beheading by the Romans in A.D. 272—an old manuscript states—"his spirit rose up and took the bleeding head in its hands and strode all the way from Paris to the place now called St. Denis, the country people much marvelling at the ghost of the saint as he strode along."

HEADLESS HORSEMAN

The tradition of the headless horseman is very ancient and examples of these phantoms can be found in the earliest German and Scandinavian folklore. Both rider and horse are said to be pitch black in color and they can just as easily gallop in the sky as on the ground. The horsemen are sometimes said to be outcasts from the Wild Hunt, or otherwise great chiefs who had the misfortune to lose their heads in battle or were beheaded. A well-known

The headless ghost of St. Denis, which terrified the people of Paris in A.D. 272

The terrifying spectacle of a headless horseman as depicted in Captain Mayne Reid's famous novel set in Texas, *The Headless Horseman* (1869)

example is the Headless Rider of Castle Sheela in Ireland, whose story is told in *Ghosts in Irish Houses* by James Reynolds (1947). Perhaps the most famous book on the topic is *The Headless Horseman,* by Captain Mayne Reid (1818–83), published in 1869 and based on an allegedly true case from Texas that the author himself had investigated. The illustration here is taken from an early edition of this popular ghost book.

HEARN, LAFCADIO (1850–1904)

The curiously named Lafcadio Hearn played a major part in revealing the mysteries of the supernatural in China, Japan and the Far East as a result of having spent the closing years of his life in that part of the world. Born on a Greek island, he spent a number of years in Ireland, England and America before moving to the Orient. He early developed an interest in the supernatural and the macabre, and the stories in several collections of his work such as *Fantastics* (1914) demonstrate his fascination with ghoulish subjects. From his later research into the lore and legends of the East came such important works as *Some Chinese Ghosts* (1897) and *In Ghostly Japan* (1899).

HELL HOUNDS

Ghostly packs of dogs, believed to be part of the Devil's hunting pack, are found in traditional legends all over Europe. These spectral creatures are said to be omens of death, and it is enough to hear their terrible howling without actually seeing them for this prophecy to come true. The most famous of these packs is probably in England, the Headless Hounds of Dartmoor. One legend says the ghost of Sir Francis Drake has been seen driving a hearse into Plymouth at the head of these fearful-looking beasts. The most dangerous of all the packs is said to be the Devil's Dandy Dogs that roam about Cornwall and are described by Robert Hunt in his *Popular Romances of the West of England* (1865).

HELPIDIUS, DEACON

According to an ancient manuscript, *Monumenta Germaniae Historica,* a certain Deacon Helpidius was the first person on record to suffer the attacks of a poltergeist. The deacon, who served as a spiritual and medical adviser to King Theodoric (son of the founder of the Ostrogothic monarchy), was apparently beset by "diabolic infestation" about the year 530. He complained that a ghostly spirit frequently bombarded him with showers of stones within his own house. As a result, a holy man was summoned to the house, he blessed it with holy water, and the deacon was troubled no more.

HERNE THE HUNTER

Herne the Hunter is one of England's most famous ghosts and is said to gallop on horseback through Windsor Park. According to tradition he was a forest keeper during either the fourteenth or fifteenth century who hanged himself on an oak tree for fear of being disgraced for some offense he had committed. On the night of his suicide a terrible storm broke out, a blast of lightning struck the tree, and the spirit of Herne was freed forever to ride about the forest. Since then Herne has been immortalized in Shakespeare's *The Merry Wives of Windsor* (1599) and in particular in W. Harrison Ainsworth's romance, *Windsor Castle* (1843), where he is pictured by George Cruikshank and described as "a wild, spectral object, possessing a slight resemblance to a human being, clad in the skin of a deer and wearing on its head a sort of helmet, formed of the skull of a stag, from which branched a large pair of antlers. It was surrounded by a blue phosphoric light." For many years a tree that stood in Windsor Park was said to be Herne's oak, but this has long since disappeared, although reports of the wild hunter himself have continued right into the present century.

HITCHHIKER GHOST

The most widely told current ghost tale in this country—according to William Oliver Stevens in his *Unbidden Guests* (1949)—is the story of the hitchhiker. According to this, someone driving a car picks up a young woman trying to thumb a ride. She accepts the lift gratefully, and asks to be set down near a certain home on the route. She chats pleasantly with the driver until the car reaches the destination. At this point the driver gets out and goes up the steps of the house to ring the doorbell. For some reason the girl stays in the car. When he returns for her, he finds nobody in the car. Mr. Stevens adds, "It comes out that she had recently been killed in a motor accident on that highway near the spot where she had begged a ride. Probably almost everyone, at one time or another, has heard a variation of the story over the length and breadth of the country."

HOME, DANIEL DUNGLAS (1833–86)

D.D. Home, called "the prince of mediums," was derided on one side by people like Robert Browning and Charles Dickens, and virtually worshipped by devotees on the other. What is beyond dispute is that he was the most famous medium of his time, and unlike virtually all of his fellow spiritualists was never exposed as a fraud. Strange psychic phenomena began to happen about Home when he was still a young man, and he developed the most extraordinary powers, which attracted people to him from all walks of life, including the French Emperor and the Tsar of Russia. Perhaps the most amazing incident linked with his name occurred in 1868 when, before a

Herne the Hunter on one of his midnight rides—an engraving by George Cruikshank in W. Harrison Ainsworth's novel, *Windsor Castle* (1834)

group of amazed watchers, he rose slowly into the air, apparently lifted by spirit hands! The seances that he conducted also gave rise to strange materializations, weird lights and inexplicable knocking sounds. Home and his powers have remained an unsolved mystery to this day, the subject of numerous studies and books, and at the heart of them his own fascinating work, *Some Incidents In My Life* (1871).

HOPKINS, ROBERT THURSTON (1884–1958)

R. Thurston Hopkins was for years a dedicated ghost-hunter as well as being a professional photographer, and his wide experience of the supernatural as well as personal encounters with the unknown give a special interest to his books. Among these works, several of which contain fictional stories as well as factual accounts, are *War and the Weird* (1916), *Adventures with Phantoms* (1947), *Ghosts Over England* (1953), *The World's Strangest Ghost Stories* (1955) and *Cavalcade of Ghosts* (1956).

HORSES

Horses, like dogs, are believed to have the facility to sense the presence of ghosts. There are many instances on record of a horse repeatedly neighing outside the house where someone is dying, and also showing evidence of being terrified if taken anywhere near the building. The subject is discussed

A trick photograph showing the famous escapologist, Harry Houdini, apparently in conversation with the ghost of Abraham Lincoln

at some length in Elliott O'Donnell's *Animal Ghosts* (1913), in which he also refers to a number of Europe's famous phantom horsemen, including the English Wild Will Darrell, the German Hakelnberg and the Swedish White Rider, all of whom are cursed to ride until Doomsday.

HOUDINI, HARRY (1874–1926)

Houdini, whose real name was Eric Weiss, became internationally famous through his remarkable escaping feats. He was also for much of his life fascinated with the supernatural. He was particularly interested in spiritualism, but believed that the manifestations that occurred at seances were staged by the mediums, and indeed he duplicated many of the phenomena by purely mechanical means. After thirty years of extensive research during which time he attended innumerable seances and put various mediums through the most intensive tests, he published his book *A Magician Among The Spirits* (1924), in which he reported that he had not been able to find a single materialization that he believed was wholly genuine. The ghost photograph of Houdini reproduced here was taken by Alexander Martin of Denver in an attempt to change his mind and allegedly shows the great escapologist with the spirit of President Abraham Lincoln. Houdini scathingly denounced it as "simply a double exposure."

I

INCUBUS

The incubus, according to medieval European folklore, is an evil spirit that comes at night to seduce young women and make them sell their souls to the Devil. A ghost-like creature, it appears in the form of a handsome young man who will endeavor to beguile any unsuspecting young woman—and once he has done so will have her totally in his power. These "demon lovers," as they were sometimes called, could also materialize in the form of women to seduce young men for the same purpose. In this disguise it was known as a succubus. A good many of the creatures of legend, like elves and trolls, were believed to be the offspring of the succubus, and the only way a person being persecuted by one could drive it off was by hanging certain herbs like St. John's wort or vervain around the bed. The subject is discussed at some length in the *Encyclopedia of Witchcraft and Demonology* by R. H. Robbins (1964).

The beguiling succubus—from an old engraving published in 1801

INDIAN SHAKING TENT

The Shaking Tent of the Indian Medicine-men has been called both the most famous and most characteristic Canadian ghost story. According to legend, Indian medicine-men, or pilotois as they were called, had the power to summon up ghosts who would cause their tents to shake, and strange, eerie lights and sounds to emanate from them. Some people believed these manifestations were simply tricks caused by the medicine-men, but exhaustive investigations by a number of people, including Father Paul LeJeune, have cast real doubts on this simplistic explanation. Father LeJeune (1592–1664), who was head of the Jesuit mission to the Huron Indians and is considered the first "psychic researcher" in Canada, came to know the Indians intimately and was particularly interested in their customs. In his *Relations* (1634) he describes witnessing a number of Indian seances and seeing the strange phenomenon of the shaking tent. He also heard tales of the medicine-men being able to speak with the dead, handle fire without getting burned, and levitate at will. At the end of his enquiry he concluded, "I am persuaded that in fact there are a few among them who have communication with Demons; but the majority are only impostors, exercising their tricks to extract presents from the sick and the poor, to make themselves popular or to make themselves feared." Later investigators have continued to probe this strange phenomenon to the present day, and the story is told in some detail in *Exploring the Supernatural: The Weird in Folklore* by R. S. Lambert (1955).

INGOLDSBY LEGENDS

One of the best-known collections of ghost and supernatural stories, *The Ingoldsby Legends*, first appeared serially in 1837 in the popular magazine *Bentley's Miscellany* bearing the pen name of "Thomas Ingoldsby." In fact, the name concealed the identity of a man named Richard Harris Barham (1788–1845), then only a minor canon at a great cathedral. Such was the success of the stories and poems that mixed comic humor with a very real knowledge of the supernatural, that Barham was soon enjoying the plaudits to which he was entitled, and in 1840 the material was collected together and published as a single volume. It has continued to be reprinted and enjoy a large readership right into the present century. The best received stories among the *Legends* were "The Hand of Glory," "The Spectre of Tappington" and "A Singular Passage in the Life of the Late Henry Harris," all of which have been constantly anthologized. Another factor that undoubtedly helped in the success of this work was the marvellous illustrations by George Cruikshank, which have also been much reprinted over the intervening years.

ICELANDIC GHOSTS

In Iceland there was for many years a law on the statute books that enabled

"The Spectre of Tappington," one of the stories in the famous collection, *The Ingoldsby Legends*, by Richard Harris Barham

people being persecuted by a ghost legally to summons it before a court of law and have it bound over to keep the peace!

IGNIS FATUUS

Ignis fatuus, or "foolish fire," is the general term given to the ghostly phenomena variously known as jack-o'-lantern, will-o'-the-wisp, corpse candle, etc. These strange, dancing lights, which are said to be omens of death, have been widely reported throughout Europe and anyone foolish enough to follow one is said invariably to be led to their death in treacherous marshland. Although they are now generally believed to be caused by igniting marsh gases, legend has it that the light belongs to a ghost named Will the Smith, a man so wicked he was barred from both heaven and hell and condemned to wander lonely places with only a flickering light to show him the way. The traditions of ignis fatuus are discussed in some detail in Katherine Briggs's *A Dictionary of Fairies* (1976).

INNOCENCE GHOST

There is an old tradition in Cornwall that any woman who is seduced and deserted, and who then dies in consequence of this act, whether in childbirth or disgrace, will inevitably return as an "innocence ghost." She will haunt her seducer and after him all the members of his family for several generations. According to Elliott O'Donnell, who recounts this tradition in his *Family Ghosts and Ghostly Phenomena* (1933), this is the reason for the haunting of many old Cornish families!

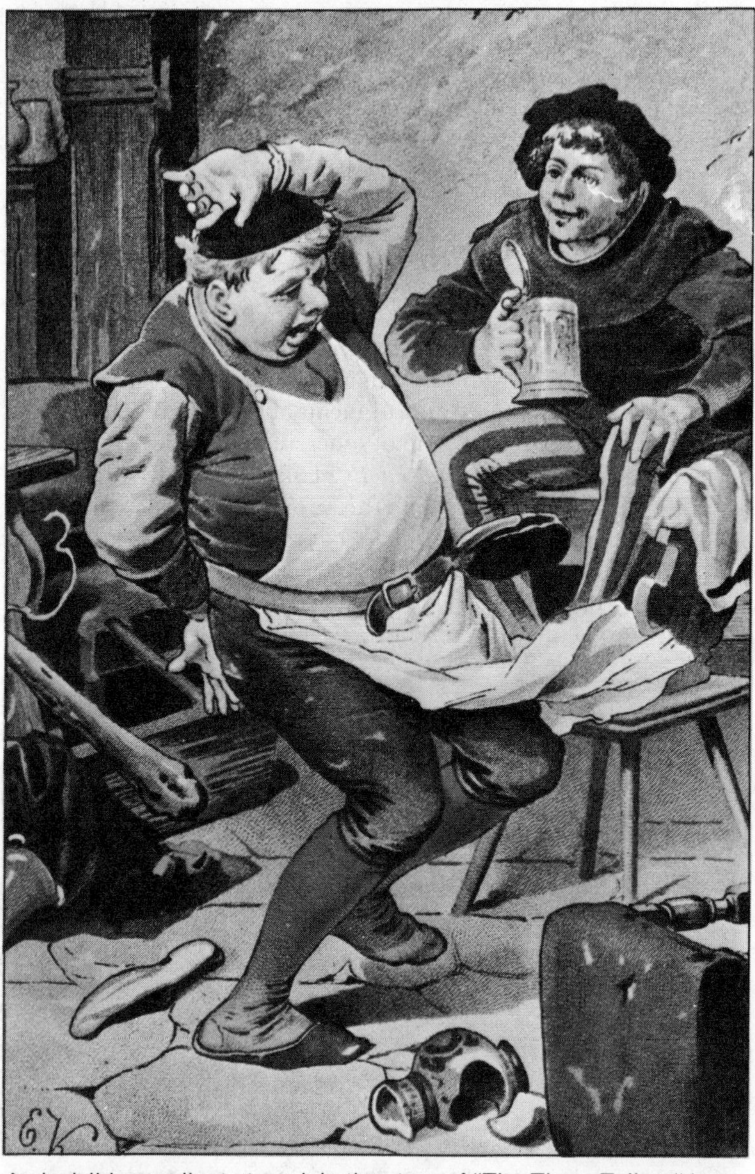

An invisible assailant at work in the story of "The Three Tailors" by the Brothers Grimm

INVISIBLE ASSAILANTS

History is full of stories of people who have been mysteriously and painfully attacked by assailants they could not see—ranging from the "invisible demon" that roamed Nanking in China in 1876 snipping off the pigtails of unsuspecting victims, to the more recent attack on the captain of a German ship in December 1931 when a four-inch wound suddenly appeared on his head before the startled eyes of his crew! Several such cases are reported in Charles Mackay's book *Extraordinary Popular Delusions and The Madness of Crowds* (1892), including one particular alarm perpetrated by a group of invisibles in Paris in March 1623 when "no man thought himself secure of his goods, no maiden of her virginity, or wife of her chastity . . . and people were afraid lest they should be turned out by the six invisibles." The whole question is discussed with a fascinating collection of other examples in *Phenomena* by John Michell and Robert J. M. Rickard (1977). See illustration on page 97.

INVISIBLES

The "invisibles" is a name that has been coined to describe the invisible playmates of many young children that only they can see. Although it is widely felt that such figures are pure figments of the imagination, it has been suggested that children have a kind of inherent power to see ghosts that the onset of maturity and the development of skepticism destroys or at least considerably weakens. Research into this subject has been conducted by the Religious Experience Research Unit at Oxford University. The photograph over of a group of children in fancy dress taken in 1928 by a Mr. A. W. Bawtree at his daughter's party, revealed an invisible playmate on the left-hand side when the picture was developed. The mysterious child was said to resemble a

An invisible child materialized on this photograph of a group of children taken in 1928

friend of Mr. Bawtree's daughter who had died suddenly a few weeks previously. The photograph was examined by numerous experts, including Harry Price, but no evidence of fraud could be detected.

IRETON'S GHOST

Red Lion Square in London, one of that city's most attractive little squares, is also famous as the place where the ghost of Henry Ireton (1611–51), Oliver Cromwell's son-in-law and dedicated enemy of the monarchy, is said to walk. According to Christina Hole in *Haunted England* (1940), the cloaked figure of Ireton sometimes has two companions, Oliver Cromwell, and another of their associates, John Bradshaw (1602–59). She writes,

> After the Restoration, their bodies were disinterred from Westminster Abbey and hanged at Tyburn as an expression of the popular detestation alike of their part in the great rebellion and of their harsh rule afterwards. There is a tradition that they were taken to the Red Lion Inn in Holborn, and this is supposed to account for their presence in that locality as ghosts.

IRVING, WASHINGTON (1783–1859)

Washington Irving, the New York writer who spent many years travelling in Europe collecting legends and folk tales, wrote a number of supernatural stories of which "The Spectre Bridegroom" and "The Legend of Sleepy Hollow," with its marvellous account of a headless horseman, are perhaps today the best known. Both were originally published pseudonymously in the *Sketch Book of Geoffrey Crayon, Gent* (1820), a work that only appeared as a result of Irving being pressed to publish it by his friend Sir Walter Scott. The two men spent much time together discussing the supernatural, and both have left important and enduring works of ghost literature.

J

JACK-IN-IRONS

Jack-in-Irons is the curious name given to a famous ghost reported to haunt the back roads of the English county of Yorkshire. He is a tall, demoniac-looking figure, swathed in chains who makes a practice of jumping out and terrifying any traveller foolish enough to be out alone at night. He is

An engraving of "Spring-Heeled Jack," the ghost-like figure who terrorized England and bears some resemblance to Jack-in-Irons

apparently one of the few ghosts who is seen wearing chains—for although chained phantoms are a favorite with cartoonists and illustrators, they are actually very rare. The reason for this is that they were the spirits of people who had died in chains when imprisoned in castle dungeons, and as this barbarous practice has long since disappeared, so have manacled phantoms. There is some similarity between him and the more widespread legend of "Spring-Heeled Jack," a mysterious figure, for a time believed to be a ghost, who terrorized the British countryside in the nineteenth century.

JACK-O'-LANTERN

Jack-o'-lantern is another name for the will-o'-the-wisp, corpse candle or ignis fatuus (meaning "foolish fire" because only a fool follows it). These ghosts take the form of small, glowing lights like candle flames, which are seen dancing in a place where it is said someone is about to die. According to legend they are all believed to be wandering souls who cannot find refuge in heaven or hell, and will lead anyone who follows them to their death. In parts of Europe they were believed to be the souls of great warriors guarding the treasure that had been buried with them. A scientific explanation that has recently been advanced to explain these spirits is that they are invariably seen where there is damp, boggy ground, and they are actually caused by the spontaneous combustion of marsh gases.

JACOBS, WILLIAM WYMARK (1863–1943)

W. W. Jacobs is the author of one of the finest and most anthologized supernatural stories, "The Monkey's Paw" (1902), a tale of ghostly sounds and a creature's paw that grants three wishes. This little masterpiece has so overshadowed all the rest of Jacobs's work that even keen readers of supernatural fiction tend to overlook his other stories of phantoms like "The Unknown," "The Interruption" and "Jerry Bundler."

JAMES, MONTAGUE RHODES (1862–1936)

Undeniably the finest ghost-story writer of the twentieth century, M. R. James was a quiet and unassuming man who spent much of his life in senior posts at Cambridge University and Eton College, buried in academic studies. Yet with thirty-odd ghost stories he showed himself the supreme master of the genre, although he considered his own skills much inferior to his mentor, the Irishman, Joseph Sheridan Le Fanu, a collection of whose finest stories James assembled in 1923 under the title *Madame Crowl's Ghost*. M. R. James began writing his stories as Christmas entertainments to be read at gatherings of fellow scholars, but in 1904 he was persuaded to publish a collection of them as *Ghost Stories of an Antiquary*, which included one of his most famous tales, "Oh, Whistle and I'll Come to You, My Lad," the title of which has now become a phrase used in connection with ghosts in the East Anglian region. A further collection appeared in 1911, *More Ghost Stories of an Antiquary*, and in time, *A Thin Ghost* (1919) and *A Warning to the Curious* (1925). All four anthologies are now much sought-after collectors' items, but the body of his work is still readily available in the much-reprinted *Collected Ghost Stories of M. R. James*, first issued in 1931. To this day, M. R. James's stories remain dramatic and chilling, with an atmosphere uniquely their own, and they are much admired and imitated by other writers in the genre.

JAPAN

Japanese ghosts are perhaps the most hideous to be found anywhere in the world, most of them being deformed and often without all or some of their

Montague Rhodes James, the master of the ghost story

limbs. The most frightening of all are said to possess either one or three eyes, have long, snake-like necks, and elongated tongues. They make a habit of haunting old houses and cemeteries. Japanese tradition says that some ghosts appear in the form of samurai warriors, complete with their battle wounds. Among all this horror, there are still the koki-teno, or fox spirits. These are ghosts that appear in the form of foxes, but have the power to change themselves into beautiful female apparitions in white, flowing robes. Not surprisingly, it is said the koki-teno can bewitch any living man who takes their fancy. For further details see Lafcadio Hearn's *In Ghostly Japan* (1899).

JIMMY SQUAREFOOT

Jimmy Squarefoot is a strange ghost, half-man and half-beast, who is said to roam about the Isle of Man. Originally Jimmy was a large, ghostly pig who was ridden about rather like a horse by a cruel giant. More recently, according to Walter Gill in his *A Manx Scrapbook* (1929), he has appeared to people as a

One of the many hideous Japanese spirits, the ghost of Sakura

A superb picture by Howard Pyle of Joan of Arc conversing with spirits

man with a pig's head and two enormous teeth-like tusks. Despite his appearance, he does no damage and would actually like to get closer to people if they would only allow him!

JINNEE

The jinnee, or genie, as it is sometimes called, is an Arab spirit, somewhat like a ghost, that is kept confined in a brass vessel or a finger ring from which it can be summoned to do the bidding of its owner. According to Julian Franklyn in *A Survey of the Occult* (1935), the jinn are a race of spirits considered to be the offspring of fire, although they can be created from a man's shadow! He explains:

> The ceremony must be performed on either a Sunday or a Wednesday night. When it has grown dark and all is still, the sorcerer lights a candle and stands facing the east with the illuminant behind him; the result of this is that his shadow is thrown large and menacing upon the wall before him. Then, in

The curious photograph of two ghosts dressed in the period of Joan of Arc which was taken in October 1925

the loneliness and silence, perhaps with a gentle draught making the magnified shadow dance and dip, elongate and grow grotesque, he addresses to it a lengthy invocation, conjuring it to depart to the home of so-and-so, and smite him in such-and-such a manner. This cantrip is repeated again and again as the candle burns away. The wax spreads, the flame gutters, the shadow darts from side to side, grows denser, denser—taller; then—out goes the light and off flies the shadow!

JOAN OF ARC'S GHOSTS

Joan of Arc, the famous "Maid of France," who claimed her actions were all inspired by ghostly voices and visions and found immortality when she raised the siege of Orleans in 1429, is now at the center of a curious story of a ghost photograph taken in a chapel dedicated to her memory. It was in October 1925 that a Lady Palmer, accompanied by a Miss Townsend, visited the Basilica at Domrémy which is dedicated to St. Joan. While admiring the British flag on display in the church, Lady Palmer was photographed by her companion. Although the two ladies were the only people in the church at

The legendary Dr. Samuel Johnson who was much interested in the supernatural and investigated the case of the Cock Lane Ghost

the time, when the picture was developed it also revealed the ghosts of two priests dressed in surplices spotted with fleurs-de-lis, the badge of the Maid of Orleans. The photograph on page 105 was subsequently examined by various experts and no evidence of fraud could be found—thus adding another small mystery to the name of Joan of Arc.

JOHANNESBURG'S UNDERGROUND GHOST

The underground tunnel in Johannesburg, which runs from the General Post Office to the main railway station, is reportedly one of the most haunted places in South Africa. During the building of the tunnel, a workman was engulfed in falling sand, and regularly since then his shade has wandered about the tunnel during the night hours. Several post office employees have recounted startling encounters with this unfortunate soul.

JOHNSON, DR. SAMUEL (1709–84)

Dr. Johnson, the lexicographer, critic and poet, whose every recorded word and gesture have become treasured by posterity was, naturally enough, interested in ghosts and the supernatural. The many studies of his life and work have made this clear, as well as his involvement in investigating the case of the Cock Lane Ghost. Two other instances cited by his friend and chronicler, James Boswell (1740–95), will perhaps suffice to underline this fact. In his *Life of Samuel Johnson* (1891) he recounts that when talking of ghosts one day, Dr. Johnson said he had a friend, "who was an honest man," who had told him he had seen a ghost. This was old Mr. Edward Cave, the printer of St. John's Gate. Dr. Johnson said Mr. Cave did not like to talk of it, and seemed to be in great horror whenever it was mentioned. Boswell then asked, "Pray, sir, what did he say was the appearance?" And Johnson replied, "Why, sir, something of a shadowy being." Boswell also quotes Dr. Johnson's considered opinion on the likelihood of ghosts: "It is wonderful that six thousand years have now elapsed since the creation of the world, and still it is undecided whether or not there has ever been an instance of the spirit of any person appearing after death. All argument is against it, but all belief is for it."

JONESBORO GHOST STORY FESTIVAL

The Jonesboro Ghost Story Festival held each October in Jonesboro, Tennessee, is a unique gathering at which amateur and professional storytellers recount factual and fictional tales featuring all aspects of the supernatural. Folk tales are particularly popular among the audience, which comprises all age groups as well as visitors from all over the world. Highlights of the weekend-long gathering are ghost stories recounted in the local graveyard, and a "tall-tale contest" in which competitors attempt to outdo each other with the most outrageous yarns.

KALGOORLIE GHOST

The famous Australian gold field at Kalgoorlie is the setting for one of the country's strangest ghost stories. Old legends tell of several ghosts that are said to haunt the heavily wooded road that runs from Perth to York and was formerly a route for the Cobb & Co. coaches, which ran to and from the gold fields. These ghosts apparently were of men who lost their lives on the dangerous ride. Not far from Kalgoorlie there was a roadside halt known as Lloyd's Inn and it was here that one of the bar girls was murdered by her lover when he discovered she was also sharing her favors with some of the coach drivers. According to the story, the girl's blood splashed onto one of the inn's walls and no matter how hard anyone tried to remove the stains, they always reappeared a few days later. Her mournful ghost also made life difficult for the owner's of Lloyd's and the haunting did not cease until the premises were finally demolished.

KANT, IMMANUEL (1724–1804)

Immanuel Kant, the German philosopher and perhaps the greatest figure in the idealist school of thought, is also important in the realms of the supernatural for his much-admired work, *Träume eines Geistersehers* (Dreams of a Ghost-Seer), published in 1766. In this fascinating volume he made one of the most-quoted observations about spirits and phantoms of the dead: "I do not care wholly to deny all truth to the various ghost stories, but with the curious reservation that I doubt each one of them singly yet have some belief in them all taken together."

KELPIE

The kelpie is Scotland's best-known ghost—a water spirit that haunts rivers, usually luring the unwary to their deaths. Although it is said that the kelpie can appear as a wild-looking man, he usually takes the form of a young horse who tricks humans into climbing onto his back and then plunges with them into the nearest stretch of water. During storms he roams about making a strange, wailing sound, and when he jumps into a river his tail is said to strike the water like the sound of thunder. The Scots have a legend that anyone who can put a bridle on this mysterious spirit can keep him as his helper for as long as he chooses. But woe betide the man should it ever be taken off, or come off—for as the kelpie makes his escape he will put a curse on his former

An evocative engraving from Immanuel Kant's work, *Dreams of a Ghost-Seer*, published in 1766

master and all his family. The kelpie is discussed in detail in *Popular Superstitions of the Highlanders of Scotland* by Stewart W. Grant (1823).

KHU

The khu was the Ancient Egyptian's word for a ghost, and it was believed to be a spirit that left a person's body as soon as he or she died. According to the tradition, these wandering spirits haunted the deceased's family and had the power to cause illness or take possession of the bodies of animals. Any person who was executed for a crime, or had committed suicide, or was drowned at sea, released a particularly malevolent khu that was much feared. To placate these evil spirits, the Ancient Egyptians would make ritual offerings to them in the form of animal flesh or rich foodstuffs. Sir Ernest Budge (1857–1934), the expert on Egyptian antiquities, has written extensively about the spirit world of Ancient Egypt in several of his books.

KIKIMORA

Kikimora was the name given by the Ancient Slavs to the ghosts that were said to attach themselves to certain households. If treated with respect, these

The ancient Egyptians' idea of a ghost, the khu, to which they made sacrifices

spirits would protect the family from misfortune and might even help occasionally in the housework by tidying up and cleaning!

KIRK-GRIM

The kirk-grim is a phantom animal that is believed to haunt old churches, according to T. Thistleton Dyer in his *Ghost World* (1893). "Sometimes it is a pig," he writes, "sometimes a horse, the haunting spectre being the spirit of an animal buried alive in the church yard for the purpose of scaring away the sacrilegious." Mr. Dyer says that it was once the custom to bury a lamb under the altar, and so if anyone enters a church out of service time and sees a little lamb spring across the choir stalls and vanish, then this is an omen that a child in the parish will shortly die. He adds that in Denmark, the kirk-grim was believed to hide itself in the church tower in order to protect the building.

KLUSKI, FRANEK (1860–1949)

Franek Kluski, a quietly spoken and rather shy man from Poland, has been called the "king of the mediums," and despite the most intensive investigation during his lifetime, none of his materializations or spirit photographs was ever proved totally bogus. Born in Warsaw, he led an uneventful life as a small-time businessman until his interest was dramatically taken with ghost materialization in the early years of this century. He attended a great many seances and was skeptical about many. In order to satisfy himself whether materialization was possible or not, he began holding his own seances—and with the most remarkable results. Independent and highly respectable witnesses who attended these gatherings left completely convinced of Kluski's extraordinary powers—and with stories of how he had materialized not only the spirits of human beings but animals as well. In his quest for truth, Kluski

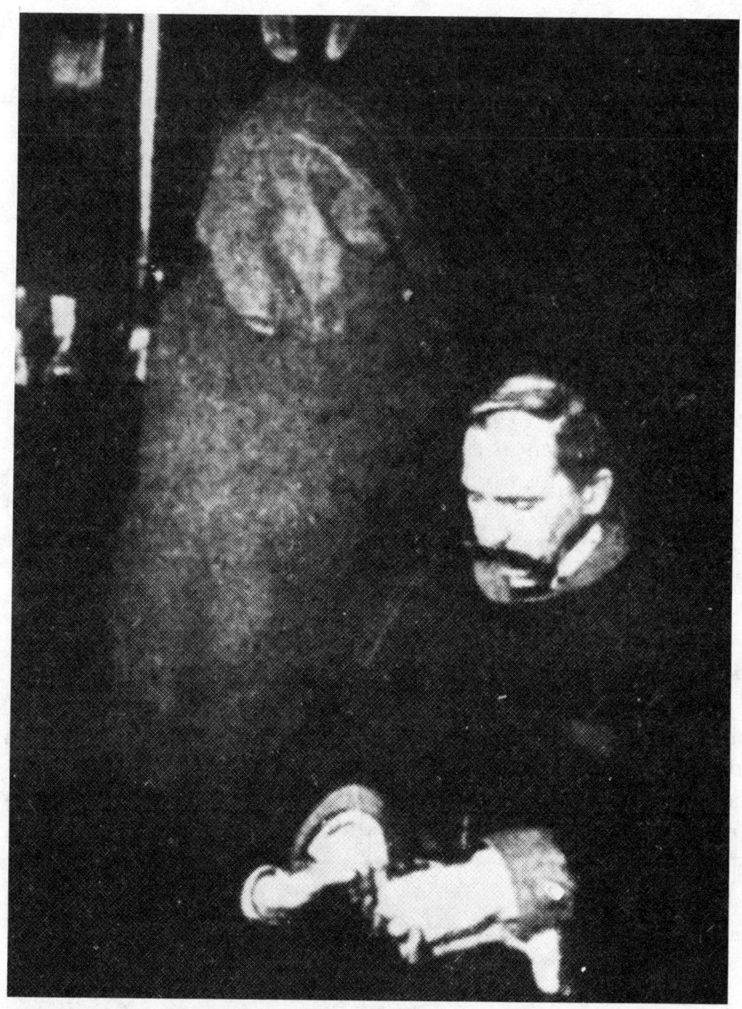

A remarkable photograph of the Polish medium Franek Kluski, materializing the phantom of a huge, shaggy ape

also developed a technique of taking wax casts of the hands of the phantoms who materialized, and though there was considerable skepticism about these, it was an undeniable fact that it would have been impossible for any ordinary people to make these casts and then withdraw their hands through the narrow wrist holes without destroying them. Perhaps the strangest and most mysterious events in Kluski's life were the materializations of a huge, shaggy creature at several of his seances between 1919 and 1922 that he called *pithecanthropus.* A remarkable photograph exists of Kluski with this uncanny phantom, and an eyewitness who was also present later wrote,

> This ape was of such great strength that it could easily move a heavy bookcase, filled with books, through the room, carry a sofa over the heads of sitters, or lift the heaviest persons with their chairs into the air to the height of a tall person. Though the ape's behaviour sometimes caused fear, and

> indicated a low level of intelligence, it was never malignant. Indeed, it often expressed goodwill, gentleness, and readiness to obey.

To this day, the mystery of what *pithecanthropus* was and how Franek Kluski materialized it has remained unsolved.

KNOCKERS

Knockers are Cornish ghosts who, according to tradition, dwell in the tin mines and indicate where ore is to be found by knocking on the walls of the shafts; hence their name. The legend says they are the ghosts of Jews who took part in the Crucifixion and were sent to Cornwall to work in the mines as their punishment. It is a fact that there were Jews working the mines in the eleventh and twelfth centuries, thereby giving a little credence to the tradition. Robert Hunt in his *Popular Romances of the West of England* (1865) says that although the spirits are basically friendly, they are frightened of the sign of the cross and therefore Cornish miners will not mark anything with this sign for fear of annoying them.

KOBOLDS

Kobolds are very similar spirits to the Cornish knockers, although legend says they are almost always evil and malicious in their intentions. They similarly live in mines, but apparently try to prevent miners from achieving their object by causing rockfalls and other small accidents.

LADY LOVIBOND

Every fifty years a terrible shipwreck which occurred on the Goodwin Sands is re-enacted by the ghostly ship and crew that took part in the original disaster. The ship is the *Lady Lovibond*, which went down with all hands on the ill-omened day of Friday February 13, 1748. According to Christina Hole, who tells the story in her *Haunted England* (1940), the tragedy happened while the master, Simon Peel, was below decks celebrating his wedding-feast. At the helm was a man named Rivers who had apparently wanted to marry Peel's bride, and out of revenge he deliberately turned the *Lady Lovibond* onto the Sands. Adds Miss Hoel, "All were drowned, and the tragic scene has repeated itself on every fiftieth anniversary since then."

LA MILLORAINE

La Milloraine, or Demoiselle, was a huge white phantom that was said to haunt the Touraine region of France. Although the shape of the ghost was always difficult to ascertain, it was widely believed to be feminine, and it only ever appeared in lonely places. La Milloraine was considered an omen of evil, and anyone who saw her was shortly to experience grievous trouble, according to the tradition.

LANG, ANDREW (1844–1912)

Though still widely known for his series of fairy-tale anthologies that have been constantly reprinted, Andrew Lang was also a serious writer on mythology and the occult as well as a tireless researcher into the supernatural. So well respected in this field was he that he wrote a number of the entries on ghosts and the occult for the ninth edition of the *Encyclopaedia Britannica* published in 1875. He also contributed an essay on poltergeists to the 1911 edition, which several authorities still cite as the best brief statement of the phenomenon. It remains a mystery to them why the entry was later deleted from the *Encylopaedia*. Among Lang's other relevant works were *Cock Lane and Common Sense* (1894), *The Book of Dreams and Ghosts* (1897) and *The Making of Religion* (1898).

LA PIERRE, JOSEPH (Fifteenth Century)

Joseph La Pierre was a French occultist who believed it was possible to "create" ghosts from the blood of people who had died. He advanced the theory that when a corpse was buried the salts it contained were given off during the heating process of fermentation. The saline particles then resumed the same relative positions that they had occupied in the living body, and a complete, if ethereal, human form resulted. This was the reason, he said, why ghosts habitually frequented graveyards—and in an attempt to prove the theory he began applying various degrees of heat to bood samples, claiming it was from this substance that the saline particles emanated. After one experiment in 1482, a report tells us,

> About midnight . . . he heard a terrible noise like the roaring of a lion. And continuing quiet after the sound had ceased, the moon being at the full, suddenly between himself and the window he saw a thick little cloud, condensed into an oval form which after, little by little, did seem completely to put on the shape of a woman and making another and sharp clamour, did suddenly vanish.

An engraving of Joseph La Pierre creating the ghost of a woman who had died by using blood from her corpse

LAVATER, LUDWIG (1527–86)

Ludwig Lavater was the author of one of the earliest books about ghosts, and certainly the first to deal with poltergeists, *De Spectris*, published in Geneva in 1570. Two years later the book appeared in translation in London under the splendid title *Of Ghostes and Spirites Walking by Nyght, and of Strange Noyses, Crackes, and Sundry Forewarnynges*, and rapidly became the principal source book on its subject for the Elizabethans. William Shakespeare, in particular, is believed to have used it as a reference book for several of his plays, especially *Hamlet*. The work covers a variety of ghostly phenomena and also contains a glossary of the different types of ghosts and spirits. Its objective and often skeptical approach to the spirit world has enabled it to retain an important place in the literature of the supernatural right up to the present day.

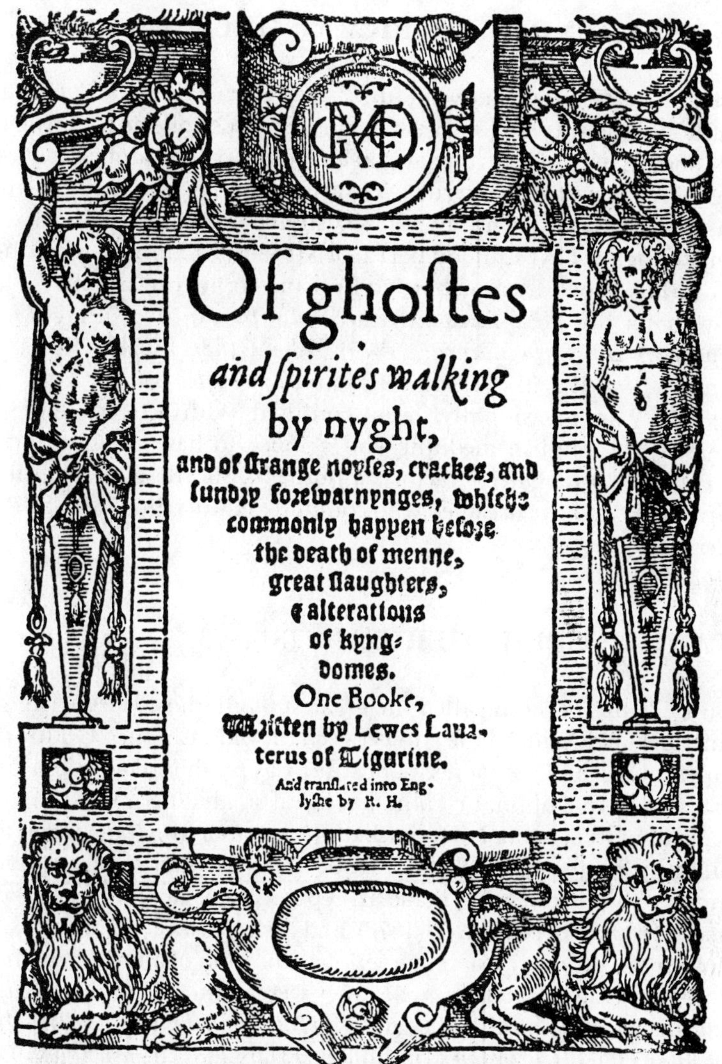
Of ghoſtes
and ſpirites walking
by nyght,
and of ſtrange noyſes, crackes, and
ſundry forewarnynges, whiche
commonly happen before
the death of menne,
great ſlaughters,
& alterations
of kyng-
domes.
One Booke,
Written by Lewes Laua-
terus of Tigurine.
And tranſlated into Eng-
lyſhe by R. H.

Title page of one of the earliest books about ghosts written by Ludwig Lavater and published in Geneva in 1570

LAZY LAURENCE

Lazy Laurence is the ghostly spirit who guards the orchards of Somerset and the West Country from all wrongdoers, human or elemental. This ghost can change his shape at will, according to tradition, and casts spells on those who trespass on his territory. An old rhyme commemorates his particular ability to cause cramps in the legs: "Lazy Laurence, let me go—Don't hold me in Summer and Winter, too." He has also been immortalized in Maria Edgeworth's story, *Lazy Laurence* (1823), which is set in the village of Aston, near Bristol.

LEE, REVEREND FREDERICK GEORGE (*c.* 1820–98)

Reverend Frederick Lee is now an unjustly neglected figure in supernatural lore although he was one of the first conscientious collectors of true ghost stories, and his five volumes of material have often proved (unacknowledged) sources of reference for later writers in the field. Lee was a hard-working and enthusiastic researcher who somehow also managed to combine this with administering the busy London parish of All Saints, Lambeth, where he was the vicar. His books are now hard to find and copies can usually be found only in major libraries. Their titles are: *Glimpses in the Twilight* (1885), *Glimpses of the Supernatural* (1875), *The Other World* (1875), *More Glimpses of the World Unseen* (1878) and *Examples of the Supernatural* (1894). He has occasionally been confused with Robert James Lee (1844–1931) the English medium who claimed to have received messages from Prince Albert, Queen Victoria's husband, shortly after the consort's death, and also to have dreamed who committed the terrible Jack the Ripper murders.

LE FANU, JOSEPH SHERIDAN (1814–73)

Joseph Le Fanu has been called the greatest of all ghost-story writers, and certainly his work bridged the gap between the old-fashioned Gothic tale of the supernatural and the modern ghost story as produced by writers like M. R. James. Born in Dublin, Le Fanu developed an abiding interest in the lore and legends of Ireland, and as a result of his research into these fields as well as collecting traditional folk tales from rural communities, he began to produce the short stories that made his reputation. Tales like "Schalken the Painter" (1880), "Green Tea" (1872) and "Mr. Justice Harbottle" (1872) display a freshness of style and marvellous evocation of atmosphere that has made them as readable today as when they were written a hundred years ago. Among his books should be listed *The House by the Churchyard* (1863), *Uncle Silas* (1864) *Chronicles of Golden Friars* (1871), *In a Glass Darkly* (1872) and *The Purcell Papers* (1880). Le Fanu's fiction takes on an added edge when one learns that, following the death of his wife in 1858, he lived as a recluse in a mood of almost constant melancholy. There have been numerous collections of his work in modern times, including a fine anthology compiled by his greatest admirer, M. R. James, the man seen as the heir to the tradition he founded. The volume is called *Madame Crowl's Ghost* (1923).

LEMURES

Lemures, or larvae, was the name given by the Romans to their evil ghosts, spirits of the dead who returned to torment their relatives and descendants. These ghosts were said to be particularly active during the month of May and

The melancholy Irishman, Joseph Sheridan Le Fanu, who wrote some of the finest of all ghost stories

regular festivals were held to propitiate them. To prevent the ghost returning of any person who it was thought might become a lemure, the Romans would burn black beans around the tomb as the body was laid to rest—for it was believed no spirit could stand the awful smell of them! The only way to drive off a lemure that did start to haunt a neighborhood was to make a terrific din with drums, for they were apparently very sensitive to loud noises!

LESLIE, BARONET SHANE (1885–1971)

An Irishman by birth, Baronet Leslie is the author of one of the classic collections of supernatural stories, *Shane Leslie's Ghost Book,* published in 1955, and reprinted several times since. A somewhat mysterious man, he spent part of his early life in Russia (where he became a friend of the writer Leo Tolstoy) and part in Europe (where he lived for a time as a tramp!). He also developed an interest in the supernatural, and painstakingly investigated a large number of cases—utilizing the most fascinating accounts in *The Ghost Book*. According to an old legend, his family was supposed to have its own banshee, which would appear to predict a death wherever the unfortunate member of the family happened to be!

LEVI, ELIPHAS (1810–75)

Eliphas Levi, known as "the last of the Magi," was a remarkable nineteenth-century French occultist credited with many supernatural powers, including the ability to summon ghosts at will. Born Alphonse Louis Constant, he was for a time a priest before being defrocked and thereafter lived a turbulent, controversial life, pouring all his hard-won supernatural learning into *The History of Magic* (1913), an essential reference work for any student of the occult. Levi was friendly with the English writer, Edward Bulwer Lytton, and appears as the magician in the latter's classic short novel, *The Haunted and the Haunters* (1859).

LHAM-DEARG

The Lham-dearg, or Ghost of the Bloody Hand, is a well-known Scottish phantom that haunts Glenmore. This unpleasant phantom has been referred to by Sir Walter Scott in his *Demonology and Witchcraft* (1830) where he writes, "There is much talk of a spirit called 'Lyerg' who frequents the Glenmore. He appears, with a red hand, in the habit of a soldier, and challenges men to fight with him. As lately as the year 1669 he fought with three brothers, one after another, who immediately died therefrom."

"The Last of the Magi," Eliphas Levi, who was said to be able to raise ghosts and was a master occultist

LIEKKIO

The liekkio is a Finnish ghost rather like the British jack-o'-lantern—a little flame that dances about in a locality where death may be expected. The word means "flaming one" and it is said to be the soul of a child who has been secretly buried in the forest.

LITHOBOLIA

"Lithobolia or The Stone Throwing Devil" is the title of a famous pamphlet published in 1698 by Richard Chamberlain, one-time secretary for the colony of New Hampshire. In it he describes how a poltergeist hurled around stones, bricks and all manner of household implements at the home of George Walton at Great Island in New Hampshire. Chamberlain himself saw the disturbances taking place—but unable to convince anyone in authority of the genuineness of the case, he was not able to publish his account until he returned to his native England in 1698. The strange occurrences, which lasted for almost three months, were at first attributed to witchcraft—hence the name given to the ghost—and it is interesting to note that this accusation was made some ten years *before* the famous witch trials in nearby Salem. The story is discussed in some detail in *Ghosts and Poltergeists* by Herbert Thurston (1953).

The Lorelei, the famous German ghost who haunts a stretch of the Rhine River

A magic lantern slide of the haunting of Lord Lyttleton by a female ghost who predicted his imminent death

LORELEI

The Lorelei is Germany's most famous ghostly spirit as well as being one of the most beautiful to be found in supernatural lore. According to the legends she is an enchanting, beguiling creature who sits on a tall rock on the right bank of the Rhine in Hesse-Nassau, singing a melody so spellbinding that it causes sailors to lose all sense of direction and steer their boats onto the treacherous rocks below her perch. The story has been immortalized in the poem "The Lorelei" by Henrich Heine (1797–1856) and the Lorelei Rock—as the nymph's perch is called—is now a favorite tourist attraction. Because of the particular rock formations in this area, it is easy to create an echo and this has often been confused with the sound of the ghost's singing. The story of the Lorelei is recounted in *The Finest Legends of the Rhine* by Wilhelm Ruland (1931).

LORD LYTTLETON'S GHOST

The account of the phantom of doom that appeared to Lord Lyttleton on November 24, 1779 at his house on Hill Street, London, and the subsequent events, comprise one of the most famous English ghost stories. Lord Lyttleton, who was something of a rake and a womanizer, was awoken from his sleep on the night of November 24 to find the ghost of a woman standing at the foot of his bed. It is believed that even in his fright, he recognized the figure as that of a Mrs. Amphlett, whose daughters he had seduced and who had died of broken hearts. Nervously he asked the spirit what she wanted, and was told that he had just three days left to live. On the following fatal Saturday, Lord Lyttleton went with a party of his friends to his other house, Pitt Place at Epsom, having told them of his experience, but describing it as merely a dream. He boasted he was in good health and would surely "bilk the ghost." Just after eleven o'clock, as he was being helped to undress by his servant William Stukey, he gave a sudden gasp and collapsed dead into the man's arms. An even stranger sequel to the story was that Lyttleton had obviously been more worried about the prophecy than he had let on to most of his acquaintances, because he had spoken seriously about the encounter to a close friend named Peter Andrews and originally planned to spend the fatal weekend with Andrews in Dartford. Instead, though, he changed his mind and went to Epsom. And at the precise moment Lyttleton was dying, Andrews was suddenly confronted in his own bedroom by a figure whom he recognized. It was his friend who cried out, "It's all over with me, Andrews." Sensing a practical joke, Andrews leapt from his bed expecting to find his friend somewhere in the house. But there was no sign of the figure and none of the servants had seen anyone entering the building. It was not until the following day that Andrews learned of Lord Lyttleton's death at the precise moment he had seen the apparition.

LUCIAN (*c.* A.D. 117–180)

Lucian, the Greek satirist, is credited with having written the first stories of a ghost club. The idea of people gathering together to relate their supernatural experiences is now a commonplace one, but it was Lucian in his humorous dialogue *Philpseudes* who first described such a group, almost 2,000 years ago! Aside from this description of what can be seen as rudimentary psychical research, Lucian also wrote exposures on fraudulent mediums, false superstitions and fake supernatural wonders.

LUCRETIUS'S SHELL

Lucretius (*c.* 99–55 B.C.) the picturesque Roman poet who is said to have died mad from the effects of a love potion given to him by his wife, was an implicit believer in ghosts and had a particular theory as to their origin. He maintained that they were a kind of shell that had diffused from the body of a dying person and thereafter persisted in the atmosphere, moving about at will. This theory is all the more interesting when considered in the light of the spiritualists' claims about the "astral body" that can leave the human frame under certain conditions—such as a trance or while a person is asleep.

M

MACHIAS GHOST

The ghost of Nelly Butler, who appeared in the home of the Blaisdel family in the village of Machias, Maine, during the year 1800, has been described as the first fully authenticated haunting in American history. An eerie, disembodied voice announced to the family in the January of that year that an apparition was going to haunt them, and then in the following month the specter of Nelly Butler appeared in the house. In the months that followed she was seen at other places in Machias, and by so many people that even the most skeptical folk had to change their opinions. Eyewitnesses said that Nelly seemed to have a shining halo around her head and could recount intimate details of people's lives when asked. However, in the spring of the following year, Nelly Butler disappeared as mysteriously as she had come and was never heard of again.

MANES

Manes was the general term used by the Romans to describe their ghosts, and they were said to be spirits who wandered about the earth interfering in the affairs of mankind in one way or another. There were two particular types of spirits: lares, who were the ghosts of people who had led virtuous lives, and lemures, who were those of wicked or criminal types. The Romans were anxious to placate these spirits as best they could and would make offerings to them known as *religiousae*. When particularly troublesome ghosts were reported, it was customary to beat drums in the vicinity of the haunting as well as to burn black beans (the Roman ghosts were apparently allergic to the noxious fumes given off) in an effort to end the disturbances. The *lares domestici* (household ghosts) were rather like poltergeists, throwing items about and pushing people, and when seen "were so ugly that nurses used the mention of them to frighten children," according to Andrew Lang in his essay, "The Poltergeist Historically Considered" (1901). The Ancient Greeks also shared a similar view of the spirit world, and mention of these ghosts is found in the works of the classical writers including Homer, Horace, Iamblichus, Livy, Lucian, Pliny, Plutarch, Suetonius and many more.

MARAS

A mara is an evil spirit that torments people at night, according to a tradition widespread throughout northern and western France. This misty form would settle on people while they were asleep and give them terrible nightmares—from which its name derived. Belief in maras is also widespread in Scandinavia, according to Elliott O'Donnell in his *Dangerous Ghosts* (1954) and in Jutland it is said that they take the form of naked woman to give men erotic as well as unpleasant dreams!

MARRIOTT, WILLIAM (1854–1938)

William Marriott was an English professional magician and illusionist who, like Houdini, devoted himself to investigating ghostly phenomena as well as exposing phoney mediums. He was fascinated by spirit photographs as well as the alleged materialization of spirits at seances, and in his quest for the truth became the scourge of unscrupulous mediums. Over and over again, he demonstrated how it was possible to fake materializations and produce even the most convincing ghost photographs. A man of great determination and a lively sense of humor, he assembled a massive collection of the equipment used by mediums to fool their customers, and posed for an amusing photograph with a selection of the disembodied hands that were a popular feature of many seances. Even such a firm believer in spiritualism as Sir Arthur Conan Doyle had finally to concede that William Marriott knew all the tricks of the ghost photographer's trade. Marriott's work was undoubtedly very important in bringing to an end the trade in spirit pictures that had deluded and defrauded so many people in the late Victorian era.

MARY CELESTE

The mystery of the American brigantine, *Mary Celeste,* which was found completely deserted sailing between Lisbon and the Azores in December 1872, has puzzled every generation since. The craft, with its sails set and moving steadily across a calm sea, was discovered by the British ship *Dei Gratia* on the morning of December 5. It was the erratic course of the vessel that attracted the attention of the *Dei Gratia,* and when it was boarded there was every indication that the crew had left suddenly and dramatically—and for a completely inexplicable reason. Half-eaten meals lay around, pipes and tobacco were left unfinished, and work was left when scarcely begun. An examination of the ship's log showed that everything had been normal until November 25—and then, *nothing.* What happened in the intervening ten days until the *Dei Gratia* came along is unknown, and not a trace of the captain or his crew has been found to this day. There have been many theories as to what might have happened, of course, but perhaps the most remarkable is the idea that a poltergeist caused the men of the *Mary Celeste* to flee their vessel. The suggestion is made by Harry Price in his book *Poltergeist Over England* (1945), and perhaps deserves more consideration than might at first be thought. "I do not remember," he writes, "ever having heard the suggestion that Poltergeists might have been the cause of the precipitate and unpremeditated flight. But that is a possibility. If Poltergeists can cause people to abandon their homes, they can make life equally unbearable

William Marriott, the English magician, with some of his props that he used to show how ghosts were faked at seances

aboard ship." He cites several other vessels found abandoned, like the French vessel *Rosalie,* discovered in 1840 and the American *Carol Deering,* which had not a soul on board in 1922, and adds, "There are records of other large vessels, all disappearing mysteriously. Are we wrong, then, in assuming that Poltergeists do not infest ships?"

"MASQUE OF THE RED DEATH, THE"

Edgar Allan Poe's famous story "The Masque of the Red Death" is said to be based on a ghostly figure that appeared among a throng of revellers at a feast held by Alexander III at Jedburgh Castle in Scotland in October 1285. This well-recorded incident describes the figure as being tall and gaunt, dressed in grave clothes, with its skull-like face hidden behind a mask. When approached, the figure disappeared in a cloud of mist leaving only the grave clothes behind.

MATERIALIZATION

The first appearance of a tangible spirit form wearing clothes—known as materialization—was recorded in New York State in 1860 during a seance held by the Fox sisters. The spirit was a "veiled and luminous female figure" and was later claimed to be the ghost of a Mrs. Livermore, the deceased wife of a New York banker. The constitution of this materialization—and those that have followed since—is said to be the substance known as ectoplasm. The first such spirit appearance in England occurred in 1872 when a Mrs. Samuel Guppy (1850–1917) caused a small white head to appear and disappear from the darkened cupboard in which she sat during her seances. This performance proved to be the model for many materializations that followed, and as the illustration here graphically shows, the "spirit" was nothing other than the medium (or an assistant) utilizing a curtain and a simple disguise to create the effect. When several mediums were caught red-handed at the trick they protested that they and the spirit form were actually connected by a kind of elastic band, and when the spirit was seized this band immediately contracted and the spirit instantly coalesced with the body of the medium! Perhaps the most famous case of materialization is that of Katie King, the spirit form allegedly materialized by Florence Cook on numerous occasions in the 1870s. An admirable study of this topic is *The Phenomena of Materialisation* (1920) by the German pioneer of psychical research, Baron Albert von Schrenck-Notzing (1862–1929).

MAZARIN, DUCHESS OF

One of the most delightful English ghost stories concerns a remarkable pact made between two royal mistresses. These ladies were the Duchess of Mazarin, who had been mistress to Charles II, and Madame de Beauclair, mistress to James II. When both had been replaced by new favorites, they became such good friends that they vowed whoever died first would make every effort to return as a spirit to the other. In fact it was the Duchess of Mazarin who passed away first, and several years later, in 1671, Madame de Beauclair was suddenly confronted by the ghost of her friend as she sat in her bedroom. According to the legend, the ghost addressed just one sentence to the dumbfounded Madame de Beauclair, "Between the hours of twelve and one this night you will be with me." And, sure enough, the two mistresses were reunited once more just as the prophecy said.

Three intriguing photographs that show how a hidden assistant could cause a "ghost" to materialize in a room and then sink into nothingness

The ghost of the Duchess of Mazarin

MESMERISM

The word mesmerism, which later became hypnotism—the art of controlling a person and making him or her open to suggestion—evolved from the activities of an Austrian doctor named Franz Mesmer (1734–1815). After forming an interest in astrology, Mesmer developed certain beliefs in the supernatural and took to holding seances. From his communications with the spirits he created a method of curing sickness by a means known as "animal magnetism," which he explained in his book *De Planetarum Influxu* (1766). His cure took the form of a large tub, filled with iron filings and magnetized water, from which projected iron rods. These were grasped by his patients and were said to effect the most miraculous cures. While many of these patients proclaimed Mesmer's system highly successful, the medical profession denounced the whole idea as bogus and he was accused of being in league with the Devil—as shown in the satirical engraving reprinted here. The whole fascinating story is recounted by L. M. Goldsmith in *Franz Anton Mesmer: The History of an Idea* (1934).

MESSAGES

Ghostly messages have been reported from as far back in hstory as the feast of King Belshazzar when a glowing hand foretold the King's doom in a message written on the wall, to the urgent appeal "Beware Titanic," which formed in shining letters on a wall and caused one passenger to deliberately avoid sailing on that ill-fated liner. There is a whole chapter devoted to luminous appearances of this kind in Charles L. Tweedale's book, *Man's Survival After Death* (1923).

A satirical cartoon on the activities of Franz Mesmer, the inventor of Mesmerism, the forerunner of hypnotism

MIDNIGHT HOUR

According to an old superstition still repeated in rural districts of Britain and several European countries, any child that is born during the "midnight hour"—between twelve and one o'clock—is said to have the power to see ghosts.

MOST HAUNTED HOUSE IN ENGLAND

Although for years Borley Rectory on the Essex-Suffolk border was considered "the most haunted house in England," Borley no longer exists and the honor undoubtedly now belongs to Sanford Orcas Manor near Sherborne in Dorset. This splendid Tudor manor house nestling in a quiet hamlet is said to be haunted by no less than fourteen ghosts! Among these are two women, one dressed all in green, and the other the Lady in Red Silk, a beguiling spirit who is said to stir just before midnight. There is also a black hound, a monk, and the ghost of Sir Hubert Medlycott, a former owner who committed suicide in the manor gatehouse. Perhaps the most bizarre is a seven-feet-tall spirit who only manifests himself when a young girl who is a virgin is present! He is said to have been a footman at the manor who made a practice of seducing the maids. Other details of Sanford Orcas can be found in Peter Underwood's *Gazetteer of British Ghosts* (1971).

MOVING COFFINS OF BARBADOS

There are a number of cases on record of coffins being disturbed by ghostly hands, but the classic case of this kind occurred during the early 1800s at Christ Church on the island of Barbados. Here, a vault belonging to the Chase family was regularly disturbed by a poltergeist between the years 1812 and 1820. Six coffins, all made of lead, which lay in a sealed vault dug out of rock, were found disturbed on no less than five occasions. The case was intensively investigated by a number of people—including the Governor of Barbados, Lord Comberemere—who could reach no other conclusion than that a violent ghost such as a poltergeist had been at work overturning and moving the coffins. In an attempt to solve the mystery, Lord Combermere conducted a rigorous test in 1819 in which he specially sealed the huge slab of blue Devonshire marble that guarded the entrance to the tomb and that required four men to move it. Prior to this the coffins had been placed in a specific order and their exact positions sketched. When, in the following April, noises were heard coming from the vault, it was speedily opened. A scene of total confusion greeted the numerous eyewitnesses, for once again the six coffins of the unfortunate Chase family had been scattered about the vault. (*See* accompanying sketches.) Rather than risk further disturbances, Lord Combermere ordered that the coffins be removed and buried in separate graves in the churchyard. Since that date there have been no further upheav-

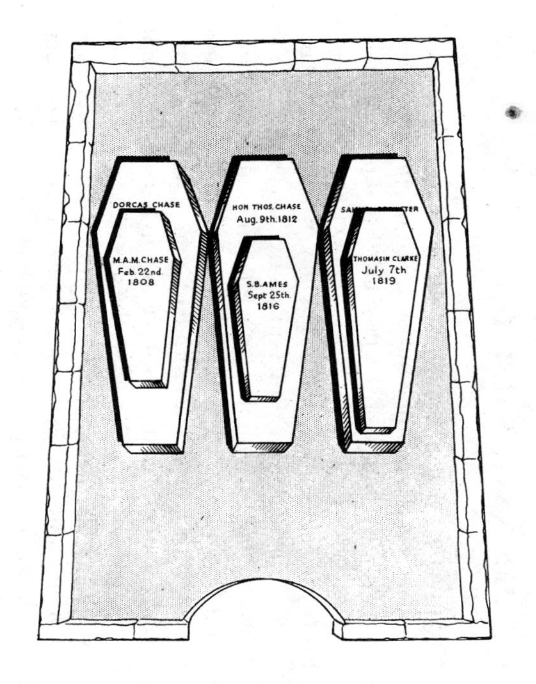

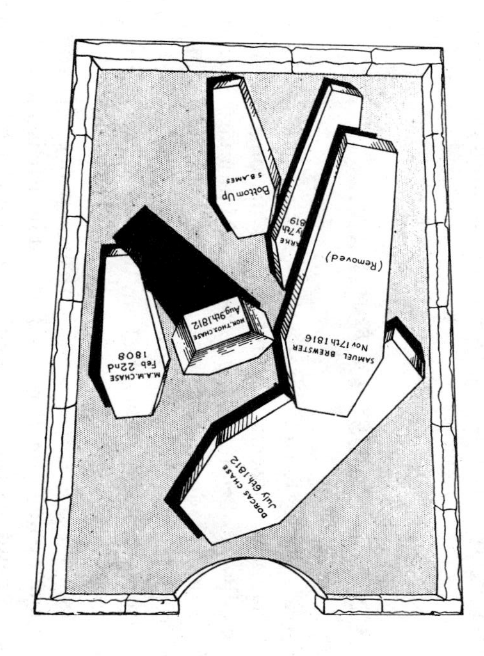

Two pictures showing the Moving Coffins of Barbados and how their positions changed from July 1819 to April 1820

als at Christ Church, but the legend of the "moving coffins" remains famous throughout the West Indies. The story has been recounted in numerous books, including Harry Price's *Poltergeist Over England* (1945).

MUMIAI

The mumiai is a particular kind of Indian ghost that is rather like the poltergeist, never showing itself and making a habit of throwing objects about or attacking people. The spirit can apparently act by day or night, and is said to make a specialty of persecuting members of the lower Indian castes who are either lazy or have criminal tendencies.

MURA-MURAS

The mura-muras are the ancestral spirits of Australia who watch over the weather, and unless they are treated with proper respect will prevent rain from falling. However, a drought can be ended by placing small stones covered with drops of blood as high as possible up in tall trees. These stones are supposed to represent the clouds while the blood signifies the rain that the people so badly need. According to Sir James Frazer in *The Golden Bough* (1890), once the mura-muras see these representations they will respond with a downfall.

N

NASEBY, BATTLE OF

The disastrous Battle of Naseby, which irrevocably ruined England's Charles I's chances of defeating the Parliamentary Army, might never have occurred if the King had listened to a ghost! According to a tradition reported in numerous studies of the English Civil War, while Charles was staying in Daventry in June 1645 he was visited by the ghost of a former supporter, the Earl of Strafford, who urged him to continue his march northwards and not to confront the superior Parliamentarian forces who were then encamped at Northampton. Charles was apparently deeply influenced by this apparition, all the more so when the Earl's ghost returned with the same emphatic message the following night. However, despite his conviction that he should not fight, Charles allowed Prince Rupert and the other leaders of his cause to

The Earl of Strafford's ghost, who visited Charles I just before the Battle of Naseby and urged him not to fight

convince him that the time *was* right to attack, and the disastrous Battle of Naseby took place on June 14. As the historian Henry Mastin notes in his *History of Naseby* (1886) if only the king had heeded the warning of the ghost and marched northwards he might have gathered more followers and then met the Parliamentarian forces on more equal terms. The illustration here of the Earl's ghost is taken from a ballad sheet of 1651 and qualifies as one of the earliest-known pictorial representations of an apparition. As a matter of interest, the headless ghost of King Charles is said to haunt Marple Hall in Cheshire, the family seat of John Bradshaw, who presided over the council that condemned the monarch to death.

NELLY LONGARMS

Although many a mother in the British Isles has cautioned her child against committing certain wrongs with the warning that if he or she does "Nelly Longarms will get you," this supposedly ghastly-looking phantom is actually pure invention, according to E. M. Wright in *Rustic Speech and Folk Lore* (1913). It is one of several "nursery bogies" invented over the years to serve as a frightening figure in which belief ceases as soon as a child grows to maturity.

NIGHT MAN

The Night Man is a ghostly spirit found on the Isle of Man who is apparently very favorably disposed towards human beings and gives warning of approaching storms by crying out or else appearing in a misty form.

NIXIES

Nixies are German water spirits not unlike the lonely Lorelei, although they can haunt any large stretch of water. They also have the ability to change their appearance at will, and can even become invisible. Legend says their normal appearance is with a human body and a fish tail, which makes them not unlike our idea of mermaids and mermen. In the main they do not bother

The ghost of a nun appearing to a woman who has evidently been dabbling in the Black Arts

human beings, although tradition says they require one human sacrifice a year and, if this is not forthcoming, they will lure an unsuspecting soul into the water and drown him or her. In the past it was said that any child born with a large head was the result of a nixie's disguising itself as a human being and marrying a normal girl.

NUGGLE

The nuggle is a relative of the Scottish kelpie and is found in the Shetland Isles where it appears as a ghostly little horse. In size and appearance it is rather like the famous Shetland ponies, but is quick and mischievous in its habits and has a distinctive tail curled up over its back. The nuggle's main purpose is to lure the unsuspecting into stretches of water—though not necessarily to drown them—and after playing its tricks it disappears in a flash of blue light. Several stories of encounters with this spirit are to be found in *County Folk Lore* by A. C. Black (Vol. III, 1901).

NUNS

According to Elliott O'Donnell in his *Family Ghosts and Ghostly Phenomena* (1933), phantom nuns are comparatively common throughout Europe, and they are believed to be the spirits of nuns who were walled up alive as punishment for some crime they had committed—usually sexual.

OCEAN BORN MARY

Ocean Born Mary is one of America's most curious ghosts, a tall, red-haired, green-eyed ghost who haunts the town of Henniker, New Hampshire. Mary received her curious name because she was born at sea, on July 28, 1720, while her mother and father were emigrating from Ireland to the New World. Her birth also occurred at a most propitious moment, for the ship on which the emigrants were sailing had just been seized by a pirate crew led by a certain Captain Pedro. However, the buccaneer was so touched by the sound of the child's cries that he promised to spare the crew and passengers if the baby was named after his wife, Mary. Happy to agree to such a simple request, the new infant was named Mary, and the pirate crew took to their ship and disappeared. Ocean Born Mary grew to be a handsome woman, much admired by the people of New Hampshire, and she also married and gave birth to four strapping sons. Later, her husband died, and when she was just about to settle into a quiet widowhood, who should come into her life but Captain Pedro, the man who had spared her life all those years ago, now pardoned and retired from the seas. According to the legend, the old sea dog and Ocean Born Mary then settled down together, both living well into their nineties. And since then, Mary's lovely ghost has returned to her home area; one suggestion is that she is looking for her second husband's hoard of treasure that he buried somewhere in the vicinity! This delightful ghost story has been retold in several books, including Hans Holzer's *Yankee Ghosts* (1966) and *Prominent American Ghosts* by Susy Smith (1967).

O'DONNELL, ELLIOTT (1872–1965)

Elliott O'Donnell has probably been the twentieth century's most prolific writer on ghosts and hauntings. Although he was born in Bristol, O'Donnell came from a very old Irish family and claimed that they were haunted by their own individual banshee! He became absorbed in the supernatural around the turn of the century, and then began to contribute stories and articles to a whole variety of magazines and newspapers. He investigated innumerable hauntings and from these experiences resulted a flood of books such as *Some Haunted Houses in England and Wales* (1908), *Twenty Years Experiences of a Ghost Hunter* (1917), *The Banshee* (1923), *Haunted Britain* (1948), *Dangerous Ghosts* (1954) and many more. If O'Donnell's claims are to be believed he visited literally thousands of haunted localities and saw hundreds of ghosts of one kind and another! He was also an enthusiastic collector of ghost photographs and published several examples he believed were genuine in his books. The picture on page 136 "The Phantom Monk," was apparently taken in an old haunted house in his home town of Bristol, and appeared in *Haunted Britain*. Shortly after his death, several collections of O'Donnell's ghost stories were republished in Britain and America, once again bringing his name to public attention.

ODYSSEUS'S GHOSTS

The epic poem the *Odyssey* by Homer contains a number of details of early man's idea of ghosts. It is an account of the wanderings of Odysseus during which time he has several encounters with spirits of the dead, "thin airy shoals of visionary ghosts" as the legendary poet calls them. Homer also wrote about ghosts in his other great work, the *Iliad*, which describes the death of Hector and the moment, "When Hector's ghost before my sight appears—a bloody shroud he seemed, and bathed in tears."

"The Phantom Monk of Bristol," a photograph that ghost-hunter Elliott O'Donnell believed to be genuine

Odysseus confronted by the spirits of the dead in Homer's classic work, the *Odyssey*

"OH, WHISTLE AND I'LL COME TO YOU, MY LAD"

"Oh, Whistle and I'll Come to You, My Lad" is the strange and eerie title of one of the most famous ghost stories in the English language, written by M. R. James (1862–1936). This superb and utterly convincing story of a haunting, which appeared in James's much reprinted book *Ghost Stories of an Antiquary* (1904), has been constantly anthologized as well as frequently broadcast and adapted for television. The story also has the unique distinction that in parts of East Anglia—where M. R. James grew up—the title is

"It Leapt Towards Him Upon the Instant," a chilling moment from M. R. James's classic story, "Oh, Whistle and I'll Come to You, My Lad"

now used to describe an old belief that it is dangerous to whistle late at night for this will cause a ghost to rise and confront the whistler.

OLD BAILEY

The Old Bailey in London is said to be haunted by a ghost that appears after particularly notorious trials have been held. The figure is said to be very shadowy, which makes it impossible to tell whether it is of a man or woman. The theory has been advanced that the ghost may be that of a prisoner sent to his or her death from the Old Bailey, while another suggestion says that the spirit could be that of a nine-year-old boy who was sentenced to death in the eighteenth century for stealing from a shop goods worth just *twopence*!

OLD BLOODY BONES

Old Bloody Bones is a curious English ghost said to haunt the area around Cornwall. According to F. W. Jones in his book *Old Cornwall* (1896) the ghost is probably one of the survivors of a terrible battle that occurred in the area, for when he is seen his thin body appears to be running with blood.

OLD LADY OF THREADNEEDLE STREET

The Old Lady of Threadneedle Street, an expression often used to describe the Bank of England in London, may well owe its origin to a ghost! Since 1836, the bank has been haunted by an apparition in black who is believed to be the spirit of a woman called Sarah Whitehead. Sarah's brother, Philip, an employee at the bank, suffered the harsh punishment of execution in 1811 for forging cheques, and this so unbalanced Sarah that she spent the remainder of her days wandering about Threadneedle Street in the hope that her brother might reappear. Following her sudden death in the street in 1836, she was buried in the bank garden, and since then she has returned every so often to continue her vain search—as well as surprising any members of the staff and visitors who have seen her.

OLD SCARF

Old Scarf is said to be an invisible spirit who roams the coastal regions of Norfolk, England, making life miserable for his victims by prodding them in the ribs or knocking them over. In a recent report Old Scarf was said to have been active in Great Yarmouth, turning an unfortunate family of holiday-makers out of their caravan!

OLD SHUCK

Old Shuck is a phantom dog well known in Norfolk, England, and other parts of East Anglia. The beast's name derives from the Anglo-Saxon *scucca*

Old Shuck, the British phantom dog, is said to have inspired Sir Arthur Conan Doyle's novel, *The Hound of the Baskervilles* (1902)

or *sceocca,* meaning Satan, and he is said to be as big as a fair-sized calf. Completely black in color (giving rise to his alternative name of Black Shuck) he pads silently about among the hedgerows beside lonely roads ready to jump out on unwary travellers. He has enormous yellow eyes that glow in the darkness as if they are on fire. It is said that anyone who meets the creature is destined to die within a year of that date. One explanation of his origin is that he is the black hound of Odin brought to East Anglia by the Viking invaders centuries ago. The legend is said to have inspired Sir Arthur Conan Doyle to write his famous Sherlock Holmes novel, *The Hound of the Baskervilles* (1902).

ONTARIO WITCH BALLS

The curious phenomena that beset the McDonald family in the little village of Baldoon in Southern Ontario is famous in Canadian ghost lore. The events began in 1829 when large pieces of timber were thrown about in farmer John McDonald's barn, to be followed by household items being dropped and smashed. When no human agency could be detected causing these accidents, it was felt that the farm must be haunted by a poltergeist. Then even more curious things started to occur—little missiles showered the house, narrowly missing members of the family. These Mrs. McDonald called "witch balls," and they convinced her beyond argument that some supernatural being was intent on harming them all. Soon sightseers were flocking to the farm, and a number of these witnessed the flying objects as well as hearing strange noises that could not be logically explained. During the next two years the disturbances continued, varying in intensity, but with no obvious explanation. The hapless McDonalds grew steadily more depressed and sought various methods of solving their problem, including calling in a "witch hunter" in the belief they were being persecuted by a witch! In late 1831, however, as mysteriously as it had begun, the poltergeist who fired witch balls at the McDonalds ceased its activities, and while the family happily returned to their former life of peace and obscurity, their experiences became part of the annals of the supernatural. Still the best account of the haunting is *The Baldoon Mysteries* written in 1871 by a member of the afflicted family, Neil McDonald, and reprinted several times.

"ON THE TRAIL OF A GHOST"

"On the Trail of a Ghost" was the title of a long, acrimonious and now famous argument that was conducted in the letters column of *The Times* of London during June 1897 about the haunting of Ballechin House in Perthshire, Scotland. The ghost appeared to be a poltergeist that filled the place with noises and made life unpleasant for the occupants. A phantom nun was also allegedly seen on the grounds. But such was the diversity of opinions about what actually happened that hardly a point about the ghost could be firmly established. With all the mounting public interest in the story, the letters to *The Times* were gathered together along with the other evidence that had been collected, and a book was issued entitled *The Alleged Haunting of B------- House* in 1899. The compilers were a Miss A. Goodrich-Freer, a psychical researcher, and Lord Bute, who had lived in the house for a period of time. If anything, this work has only served to deepen the mystery of Ballechin House for, evidently afraid of starting up the row all over again, the compilers inserted initials, dashes and dots to disguise all the real names and crucial incidents in the story! Copies of this book (which nonetheless proved popular and was reprinted a year later) still exist and make interesting if infuriating reading.

A group of people using the Ouija board to obtain messages from the dead—a still from the film, *The Uninvited* (1944)

OUIJA BOARD

The Ouija board is widely claimed to be the medium through which the spirits of dead people can communicate with the living. The Ouija—from the French *Oui* and German *Ja*—consists of thirty-eight pieces of card ranged in a circle around the edge of a polished table. On twenty-six of the cards are the letters of the alphabet, on ten of them the numbers 0 to 9, and on the last two the words Yes and No. In the center is placed an upside-down tumbler or wine glass. Those taking part then sit around the table and place their index fingers on the glass, and a question is asked. The glass then moves towards

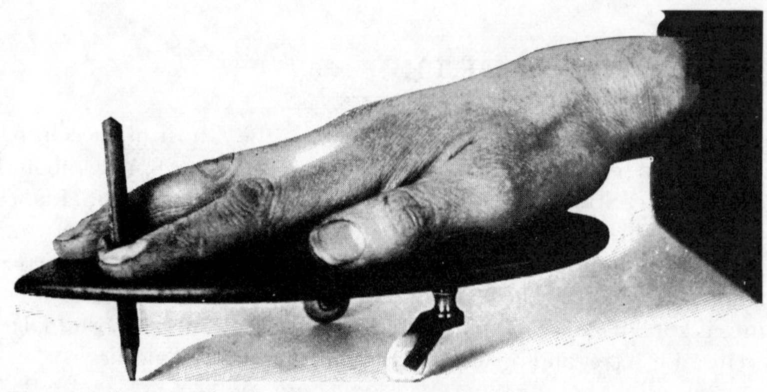

The planchette, which is also supposed to be able to record messages from the "other side"

Australia's most famous phantom, the Ghost of the Outback, which was photographed at Corroboree Springs in 1956

either the Yes or No card and if the response is positive will slide backwards and forwards around the letters and numbers spelling out the answer. Believers claim that when the glass moves it is acting as a kind of "telephone" to the spirits of people who have died. A variation of the Ouija board is the planchette (named after its French inventor in 1853), a heart-shaped piece of wood on two small wheels with a pencil providing the third arm of support. The operator places his or her hand on the planchette and, if the conditions are favorable, it will begin to move about, writing messages on a piece of paper placed beneath it. The subject is fully discussed in *On The Threshold of the Unseen* by Sir William Barrett (1918) and formed a memorable sequence in the film *The Uninvited* (1944), about the attempts of a group of four people to exorcize a ghost from their home.

OUTBACK, GHOST OF THE

One of Australia's most famous phantoms is the Ghost of the Outback, which has been repeatedly seen in a clearing at Corroboree Springs about 100 miles from Alice Springs. In May 1956, a visitor, the Reverend R. S. Blance of Tusmore Presbyterian Church, Adelaide, not only saw the short, dark-featured spirit, but took a photograph of it. His picture has lent credence to the suggestion that the ghost might be that of an Aborigine, for Corroboree Springs is known to have been used in the past by the Arunta Aboriginal tribe as a center for secret and occasionally fatal initiation ceremonies.

P

PALATINE

America's most famous phantom ship is the *Palatine,* an unearthly vessel that has been reported for over two hundred years at points along the North American coast. The phantom is all the more impressive and unmistakable because it appears to be on fire from stem to stern. According to the legend, the *Palatine* was a Dutch immigrant ship that sailed across the Atlantic to America in 1752. However, as soon as it reached the coast of the New World it ran into the most terrible storm just off Rhode Island, which battered it unmercifully and led to the death of its captain. The crew apparently then mutinied, stole everything they could lay their hands on, and took to the life boats, leaving the passengers to fend for themselves as best they could. With no crew to steer the vessel, the ship drifted helplessly for some days until it finally ran aground on Block Island. Here the exhausted and bewildered passengers struggled onto dry land at last, to be immediately confronted by a group of local inhabitants who rushed on board the ship to see what loot they could find. Frustrated at discovering nothing of value left by the mutineering sailors, they set fire to the vessel and allowed it to drift out to sea. Soon the flaming ship had disappeared over the horizon. However, on numerous occasions since—and always on the anniversary of the original tragedy—the *Palatine* has been reported once more off the same coast; still blazing just as fiercely as when she was last seen.

PEARLIN JEAN

According to Charles Kirkpatrick Sharpe (1781–1851), the Scottish antiquarian, "Pearlin Jean was the most remarkable ghost in Scotland and my terror when a child." This strange, female figure with her head and shoulders covered in blood, haunted the mansion of Allanbank at Edrom in Berwickshire. The girl is said to be the spirit of a beautiful French girl named Jean who, in the seventeenth century, was scorned by her heartless lover, Sir Robert Stuart of Allanbank, and then knocked over and killed by his carriage when he drove away ignoring her entreaties. As a result she returned to haunt him and his family. Those who first saw the ghost were in no doubt it was Jean because she was dressed in the same fine pearlin lace that she had always worn when alive. There are other reports of people hearing the rustle of Pearlin Jean's silks in the vicinity, although not actually seeing her.

PEG O'NELL

A headless stone figure on the grounds of Waddow Hall near Clitheroe, England, commemorates Peg O'Nell, an evil spirit who haunts the nearby River Ribble. According to tradition, Peg O'Nell was a servant at Waddow Hall who quarrelled with her mistress and after her own death returned as a malevolent phantom. She also left a curse on the Hall that every seven years she would claim a victim in the River Ribble. For a time it was said locally that a cat or dog used to be drowned on Peg O'Nell night to avert this tragedy. The story of this ghost is told in *Folk-Lore of the Northern Counties* by William Henderson (1879).

PERFUME GHOSTS

English researcher Edith Cave is convinced that ghosts often appear in the form of a phantom scent in the air. As a result of a nationwide survey in England in 1978, she published numerous cases of people who had suddenly become conscious of a smell that was instantly identifiable with someone who had died. Among these she quoted the instance of a Bristol woman who could smell the perfume her mother used to wear wafting along the stairs of her house, while a man in Okehampton, Devon, said he awoke one day to "the most beautiful, unexplained perfume—I felt completely peaceful and unfrightened." It was just three weeks after his father had died. More curious still, Mrs. Cave quotes the case of a mother in Ross-shire, Scotland, who said her baby son had died after falling into a sheep dip, and then at least once a week afterwards the whole house was pervaded by the smell of chemical dip. And a Northampton couple reported that they often smelled aviation fuel after their son was killed in an air crash. John Aubrey in his *Miscellanies* (1696) gives perhaps the most famous historical instance of a ghostly scent. "*Anno 1670*" he writes, "not far from Cirencestor, was an apparition. Being demanded whether a good spirit or bad, it returned no answer, but disappeared with a curious Perfume and most melodious Twang." At the turn of the century, an American illusionist named F. L. Jossefy used to materialize a ghostly figure known as "the spirit of the flowers," which he claimed was part spirit and part perfume. A photograph of this ghost is reproduced here.

PERKS, THOMAS (*c.* 1680–1703)

The story of the young gunsmith, Thomas Perks, who attempted to raise spirits of the dead and drove himself mad, is another famous ghost story. Perks became fascinated with astrology and acquired an old book of magic spells, one of which gave instructions for raising ghosts. One night he drew the requisite ritual circle at a crossroads and, according to Lionel A. Weatherly in *The Supernatural* (1891), "the spirits appeared faster than he desired, and in most dismal shapes, hissing at him and attempting to throw spears

"The Spirit of the Flowers," a ghostly figure materialized by the American illusionist, F. L. Jossefy

and balls of fire, which did very much affright him, and the more so that he found it was not in his power to lay them, insomuch that his hair stood upright, and he expected every minute to be torn to pieces." These spirits apparently trapped the unfortunate Perks in his circle until daybreak, after which, says Weatherly, "he never recovered from the shock, and pined away and died." This story has been repeatedly cited as a warning to all those who attempt to contact the spirits of the dead. See illustration on page 146.

PHANTASMAGORIAS

Ghost-making machines, or phantasmagorias as they became known, were one of the most popular forms of public entertainment in the closing years of the eighteenth century and also through much of the nineteenth century. The principle of using apparatus like a magic lantern to project ghostly figures before an audience—the basic idea of the phantasmagoria—had been known since the fifteenth century, but it was thanks mainly to the work of a Belgian optician, E. G. Robertson, in the 1790s, that the "ghost illusion" became both convincing and popular. As one commentator wrote in 1798: "Go to Robertson's exhibition and you will see the dead returning to life in crowds.

The unfortunate Thomas Perks whose attempt to raise the spirits of the dead led to his own death

Robertson calls forth phantoms and commands legions of spectres." So convincing were the ghost-making machines that once the techniques had become understood by unscrupulous operators they were being put into use to "raise" the spirits of departed relatives for gullible clients. Scores of these men, who said they could bring back the dead, flourished throughout Europe, and it took a concerted effort by the authorities in several countries to prove they were using trickery before the public would give up being so easily

A revealing sketch that demonstrates how ghosts were produced in theaters by use of the phantasmagoria equipment

parted from their money. The story of the phantasmagoria, the work of Robertson and his successors' including the talented British exhibitor Professor John Henry Pepper, as well as the exploitation of the ghost-making machines, is fascinatingly recounted in *The Wonder of Optics* by F. Marion (1868), from which the revealing illustration here is taken. The author of this dictionary has also covered the story in his own book *Ghosts: An Illustrated History* (1974).

PHANTOM ARMIES

No doubt as a result of the awful carnage of battle, phantom soldiers and ghostly armies have been reported throughout history. The earliest such stories date from the days of the ancient Assyrians, when ghostly warriors were said to have made attacks on desert cities, and they go right through to the recent war in Vietnam, when the footsteps of a ghostly platoon baffled a group of American soldiers in 1971. It is said that on certain nights of the year knights in armor can be heard at Glastonbury, and there have been continuing reports over the years that uniformed men have been seen on Marston Moor, both in England. The First and Second World Wars have produced the largest number of ghost stories and interesting selections of them are to be found in *War and the Weird* by Forbes Phillips and R. Thurston Hopkins (1919) and *Strange Mysteries of Times and Space* by Harold T. Wilkins (1958).

A superb illustration by Virgil Finlay for one of the finest short stories about a phantom army, "Three Lines of Old French," by A. Merritt

PHANTOM BELLS

The ringing of phantom bells that once tolled in churches now submerged off the coast of the British Isles is a commonly recorded phenomenon according to Alasdair Alpin MacGregor in his *The Ghost Book* (1955). He cites two famous examples, Dunwich, the once prosperous city that now lies under the waves off the Suffolk coast, and the drowned land of Lyonesse off the Cornish coast. Many people living on the coast near these two sites have heard bells pealing when stormy weather is due and, in particular, at Christmas time. MacGregor says the people always check after hearing the sounds to make sure no church bell on land was ringing at this time, and they say the final proof that the tolling came from a phantom bell is that there is always a note missing. Apart from other phantom bells reported issuing from drowned churches in lakes in Wales, Scotland and Ireland, MacGregor adds,

> Legends and traditions of drowned cities, of submerged towns are current over all the world. On the European continent they are numerous, particularly in France, Switzerland, Germany and the Baltic Islands. With many of them is associated the ringing of ghostly chimes. The bells of Gelte, a village near Themar, in Germany, long since submerged, are often heard pealing at midnight. So also, at certain times of the year, are the bells of the drowned city of Boisse, heard by travellers passing between Niort and and Fontenay.

In his book *Strange Things Among Us* (1895), H. Spicer quotes several examples of English families haunted by phantom bells that ring shortly before someone in that family is about to die. These sounds can either come from bells inside the house that no human hand has touched, or else from church bells that ring of their own accord. The most famous instance of a family haunted by a bell sound that could never be traced were the Pine-Coffins of Portledge in North Devon, whose story is related in *Apparitions: A Narrative of Facts* by Revd B. W. Saville (1905).

PHANTOM BIRDS

There are a number of instances of ghostly birds appearing at the bedsides of people in the last stages of dying, perhaps the best account of this being a seventeenth-century pamphlet entitled "A True Relation of an Apparition in the likeness of a BIRD WITH A WHITE BREAST, that appeared hovering over the death bed of some of the children of Mr. James Oxenham of Orehampton in Devon." The work describes how this phantom bird, which had been reported as early as the previous century, invariably made its appearance whenever a member of the Oxenham family lay dying. Other birds of this kind include the owl that haunts the Arundel family of Wardour, the swan with a blood-stained chest that appears to the Kirkpatricks of Closeburn Castle, and a beautiful, ghostly robin, which has been reported several times in Durham.

The phantom swan of Closeburn Castle, whose appearance heralds a death in the Kirkpatrick family

PHANTOM COACH

According to tradition, the phantom coach comes to fetch the dying, as well as being used by the dead for late-night drives. It can either be a genuine coach or else a hearse, but it is always black like its driver and horses, and they are almost always headless. Rarely does the coach make any sound, but it travels at great speed, and for anyone to see one is said to be an omen of death. These coaches are believed to have superseded the bands of phantom huntsmen who once plagued the countryside, according to an anonymous writer in the *Athenaeum* in 1847. He writes,

> The spectral appearance often presents itself in the shape of a great black coach, on which sit hundreds of spirits singing a wonderfully sweet song. Before it goes a man who loudly warns everybody to get out of the way. All who hear him must instantly drop down with their faces to the ground, as at the coming of the wild hunt, and hold fast by something, were it only a blade of grass; for the furious host has been known to force many a man into its coach and carry him hundreds of miles away through the air.

Phantom coaches have apparently become rarer since the advent of the motor car, but they are still being reported in parts of rural England as well as in France and Germany. Perhaps the most famous phantom coach is the Tur-

Nineteenth-century picture of the phantom coach, which is said to be an omen of death to anyone who sees it

berville Coach of Dorset, which runs at dusk from Woolbridge Manor, the ancient seat of the Turberville family, to a point near Bere Regis. It is said only to date from just over two hundred years ago, but is still an omen of death to anyone who sees it. The phantom was immortalized by the great English writer Thomas Hardy (1840–1928), who knew the legend well and makes mention of it in his famous work *Tess of the d'Urbervilles* (1891). Like a number of phantom coaches, it is believed to owe its origin to a terrible murder. Another famous coach is that belonging to Sir Francis Drake, which he is seen driving across Dartmoor on starless nights, followed by a pack of baying hounds.

PHANTOM HEADS

There are many instances of hauntings by disembodied heads in both Europe and America, perhaps the best authenticated account coming from Oakland near San Francisco, and reported in 1891. According to the *San Francisco Examiner* a family named Walsingham was haunted by a phantom head that first appeared as a spherical eerie light and gradually developed into a head with long, gray, matted hair and bloodstains on the forehead. The head floated about six inches above the floor, but as soon as anyone approached it he or she had the sensation of icy fingers choking his or her throat. Several outsiders stayed in the house and both saw and felt the head. Such was the terror that it caused that the house was evacuated and eventually pulled down. When a headless skeleton was discovered in the foundations, local gossip believed the cause of the haunting had been found. Elliott O'Donnell devotes a fascinating chapter to phantom heads in his *Dangerous Ghosts* (1954).

PHANTOM SHIPS

The *Flying Dutchman* (which is referred to in a separate entry) is the most famous of the many phantom ships that are said to sail the world's oceans as well as haunting the coasts of many nations. A famous eighteenth-century poem captures the essence of the belief in these ghostly vessels:

> 'Tis the phantom ship, that in darkness and wrath,
> Ploughs evermore the waste ocean path,
> And the heart of the mariner trembles in dread,
> When it crosses his vision like a ghost of the dead.

Stories of phantom ships appear in the folklore of France, Germany, Denmark, Ireland, England, Scotland, Canada, America and even China, while earlier tales appear in Hindu, Norse and Russian legends. According to T. R. Bassett's *Legends and Superstitions of the Sea* (1924) there are famous phantom vessels in the Baltic and Sargasso Seas, and another ship the size of a mountain that scraped the cliffs of Dover while it was squeezing through the English Channel! Raymond Lamont Brown also provides a fascinating survey of modern ghost ships in his *Phantoms of the Sea* (1972), in which he

A phantom ship as illustrated in *Legends and Superstitions of the Sea* by T. R. Bassett (1924)

describes such extraordinary accounts as the "Ghost Ships of the Goodwin Sands," the American "Case of the Headless Sailor" and "The Kaiser's Haunted Submarine." He also devotes an interesting section to "Voices From the Sea" about the strange sounds of drowned sailors like "Yorkshire Jack," whose cries have been heard for generations.

PHOUKA

The phouka, or puca, is another of Ireland's famous ghosts, and is mostly seen in the form of a horse, though he can appear as a goat, an ass, a bull, and even an eagle or a bat! The name is believed to derive from the word *poc,* a he-goat, and it has been suggested that he was the forefather of Shakespeare's Puck. He lives in isolated mountains or among old ruins, and there are a number of places in Ireland known as "poula phouka" of the "hole of the phouka." The best known of these spots is a waterfall of this name formed by the Liffey in County Wicklow. The ghost's main purpose seems to be to carry off unsuspecting victims for wild rides across the countryside, having first crept up behind them and tossed them onto his back. Country people still warn their children that they should not pick and eat blackberries after Michaelmas Day (September 29), as the decay that begins to affect them at this time has been caused by the phouka. In some parts of Ireland the spirit is said to be more mischievous than dangerous, and in the main helpful and well-disposed towards humanity—as long, that is, as he is treated with respect. As historian Douglas Hyde (1860–1949) has written in *Beside the Fireside* (1920),

> In an old story we read that "out of a certain hill in Leinster, there used to emerge as far as his middle, a plump, sleek, terrible steed, and speak in human voice to each person about November-day, and he was accustomed to give intelligent and proper answers to such as consulted him concerning all

The phouka, or puca, the Irish ghost that appears in the form of a horse and carries off the unwary in a madcap ride!

that would befall them until the November of the next year. And the people used to leave gifts and presents at the hill until the coming of Patrick and the holy clergy." This tradition appears to be a cognate one with that of the Puca.

PLANET OF DEATH

The planet of death is supposed to be a sphere where gather the departed souls of people who were too wicked during their lives to be reincarnated. On the planet, says an entry in *A Survey of the Occult* (1935), these spirits, which are not even to be allowed to return as evil ghosts, are finally destroyed.

POLTERGEIST

The poltergeist is both one of the most famous and least attractive of ghosts. Its name is a compound of the German verb *polter,* to make a noise by knocking or tumbling things about, to knock or rattle, to scold or bluster, and the noun *Geist,* a ghost. (There is also a similar English description of the spirit as being a polterghost, deriving from the verb *polt,* to knock, thrash, beat and bang, but this has mostly been ignored in favor of the German word.) The poltergeist is invisible and has a complex character that is best described by the great expert on the subject, Harry Price, in his exhaustive study, *Poltergeist Over England* (1945):

> A Poltergeist is an alleged ghost, elemental, entity, agency, secondary personality, "intelligence," "power," spirit, imp, or "familiar" with certain unpleasant characteristics. Whereas the ordinary ghost of our story-books is a quiet, inoffensive, timid, noiseless, and rather benevolent spirit, with—usually—friendly feelings towards the incarnate occupants of any place where it has its abode, the Poltergeist is just the reverse. According to the many reports of its activities, in all lands, and in all ages, the Poltergeist is mischievous, destructive, noisy, cruel, erratic, thievish, demonstrative, purposeless, cunning, unhelpful, malicious, audacious, teasing, ill-disposed, spiteful, ruthless, resourceful, and vampiric. A ghost *haunts,* a Poltergeist *infests.* A ghost likes solitude, a Potergeist prefers company. A ghost seeks the half-light; a Poltergeist will "perform" in sunlight.

An interpretation of the activities of a poltergeist by Harry Price based on his researches

Simplified, the poltergeist has come to be known as a "racketing spirit" that is almost invariably associated with a young adolescent, either a boy or a girl. This association has naturally led to many stories of poltergeists being dismissed as the secretive activities of these youngsters. Another theory has also been advanced that poltergeists need the particular energy of the young to be able to function. As Harry Price has written further,

> Poltergeists are able, by laws as yet unknown to our physicists, to extract energy from living persons, often from the young, and usually from girl adolescents, especially if they suffer from some mental disorder. They are able, by some means, and by using these young people as a fulcrum, lever, or support, to increase and nourish this energy, and to direct intelligently this power. They are able to use this power telekinetically for the violent propulsion or displacement of objects, for purposes of destruction, and especially for the production of every variety of noise—from the "swish" of a silk skirt to an "explosion" that makes the windows rattle.

POLTERGEIST, LEGAL

The story of the poltergeist that won legal status in the British Courts is now largely forgotten. In the early years of this century, the English poet, Stephen Phillips (1864–1915) took a secluded house near Windsor in which he hoped to find the peace and quiet to work. Within days, however, he was being plagued by unaccountable noises; footsteps were heard about the house, doors opened and closed without reason, and cries of terror and despair resounded throughout the building. Unable to work amidst such a din, Phillips quit the house and soon his experience was being recounted in the press. The owner of the house felt outraged at this publicity and sued two of the newspapers concerned, winning his case and being awarded damages. However, when one of the papers appealed against this decision, the appeal was upheld in the High Court. Although never called into the witness box, the poltergeist of Windsor had earned itself a place in legal history!

POOLS OF DOOM

Supernatural lore contains numerous instances of haunted pools—stretches of water that seem to exude a feeling of profound sadness and depression. Some are even said to attract a certain kind of ghost, usually mischievous spirits and those inimical to humans. A number of such pools, usually known as "death pools," are described by Elliott O'Donnell in his *Haunted Britain* (1948), where he advances the theory that most of them have earned their sinister reputations by being used by suicides for drowning.

PRICE, HARRY (1881–1948)

Popularly known as "the ghost-hunter," Harry Price was a colorful and industrious psychical researcher, who only occasionally marred the importance of his work by deliberate sensation-seeking and showmanship. His investigations into various aspects of the supernatural, and in particular his detailed study of Borley Rectory in Essex, "the most haunted house in England," made him world-famous. He was particularly interested in fraudulent mediums and psychic photography, and as a result of his research assembled a huge library of rare and important books, magazines, pamphlets, scrapbooks, illustrations and photographs, which is now housed at the University of London. Price's life and activities have been retold by Paul Tabori, his literary executor, in *Harry Price—The Biography of a Ghost Hunter* (1950), and among his own works should be mentioned *Leaves From a Psychist's Case-Book* (1933), *Confessions of a Ghost Hunter* (1936), *Fifty Years of Psychical Research* (1939) and *Poltergeists Over England* (1945).

A curious photograph of ghost hunter Harry Price complete with a spirit form. Needless to say, it is a fake

PSYCHOGRAPHS

Psychographs—or scotographs—were another supernatural curiosity much in evidence at the turn of the century. They were photographs on which appeared ghostly messages from people who had died—or at least that is what the photographers who took them claimed. The blurred and often illegible words appeared on photographs of relatives who posed in the hope of being contacted. As long as they had the money to pay, said the skeptics, they received a message of sorts. Where messages from famous people were sought—and it was possible for the photographer to get hold of samples of that person's script—the handwriting dramatically improved and became

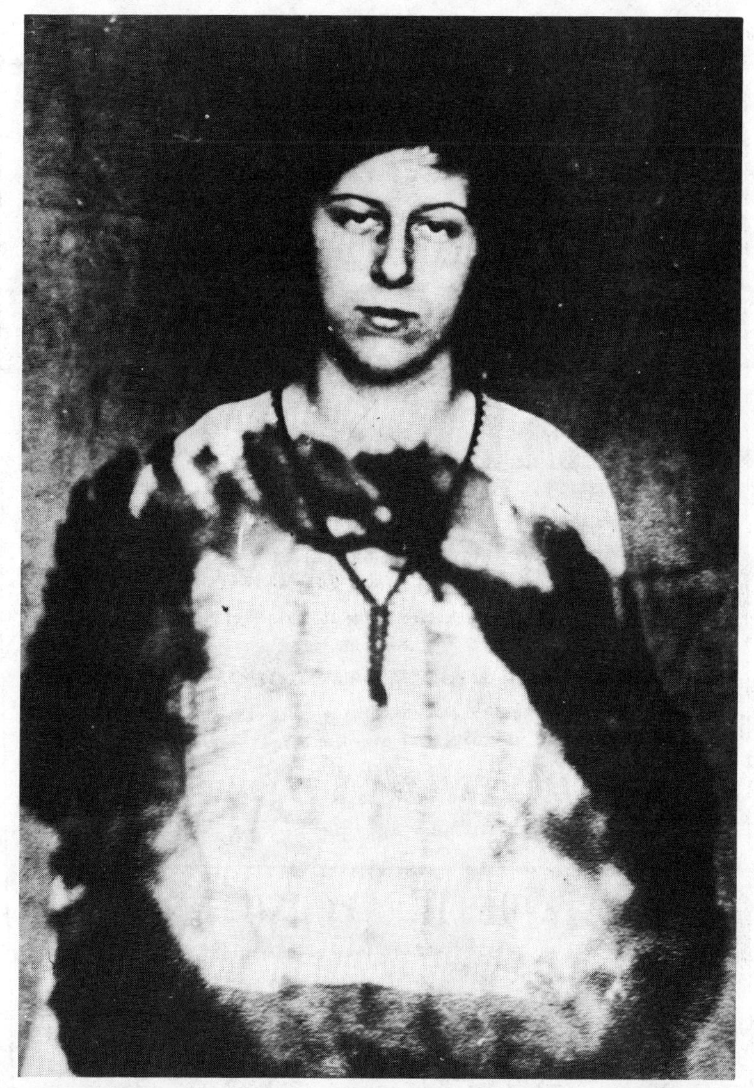

A typical example of a psychograph—a photograph containing a ghostly message—and certainly a fake

quite legible and the words understandable. The subject has been discussed and various other methods of perpetrating the fraud explained by the photographic expert, Fred Barlow, in his *Ghost Photographs* (1923).

PSYCHOMANCY

Psychomancy is the ancient art of divination by ghosts; the reading of future events, in particular those of death and misfortune, from the appearance of the spirits of the dead.

THE HISTORY OF THE

Mysterious House

And alarming Appearances

AT THE CORNER OF STAMFORD ST., BLACKFRIARS ROAD,

Well known to have been unoccupied for many Years, and called

The Skeleton's Corner!

ALSO THE PARTICULARS OF THE

FEMALE SPECTRE

Which appeared at the Window;

And an account of who are the

VICTIMS OF SEDUCTION AND MURDER.

The wonder and excitement caused by the appearance of the house, and also by the curious and

Extraordinary Disappearance of the Inmates.

Alarming noises and strange shadows; the curiosity exited on passing the house, and an account of what has been reported to have been seen of the

Skeleton and Apparitions.

THE REPORT OF THE BUTCHER, BAKER, AND THE PIEMAN,

And other interesting particulars. Spectre visit of that strange Female in Black, and

FATE OF THE YOUNG LADY

Supposed to be a tenant many years ago; also an account of an old haunted Mansion in the country, and the courage displayed by a young Officer.

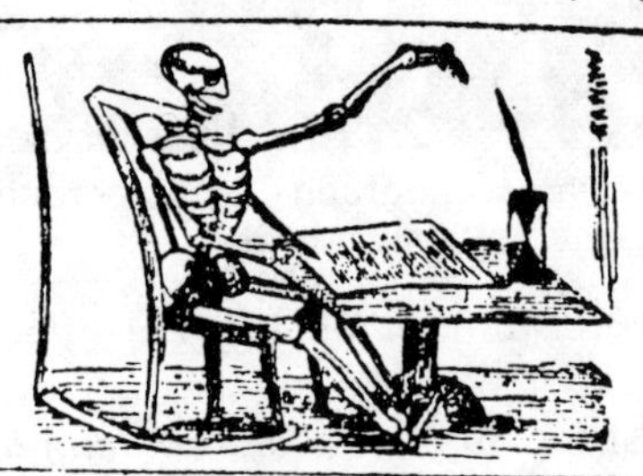

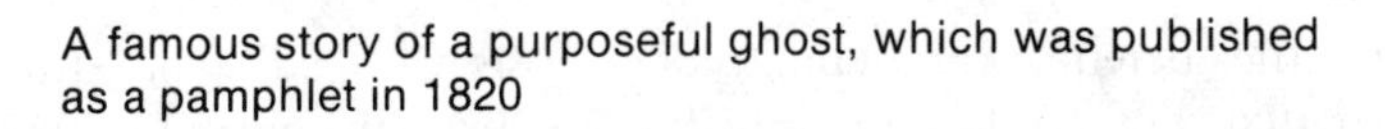

LONDON: PUBLISHED BY W. JENKINSON, 91, LEATHER LANE, HOLBORN,

And Sold by all Booksellers.

A famous story of a purposeful ghost, which was published as a pamphlet in 1820

PURPOSEFUL GHOSTS

Folklorist Christina Hole devotes a whole chapter in her book *Haunted England* (1940) to the type of short-lived ghosts who return with a purpose in their haunting. She writes:

> Some ghosts return only for a brief space, to give a message or redeem a promise, and then, their mission fulfilled, vanish for ever from this world. Some pre-occupation with earthly affairs has detained them for a little and once they have rid themselves of it, they have passed on to the next stage of that journey of which death is only the beginning. The murdered have returned to bring their murderers to justice; the wealthy have appeared to ensure the right disposition of their property or to reveal the hiding-place of treasure. Or a wrong done may bind the spirit till it has been righted. Whatever the original cause, the haunting has ceased once the necessary knowledge has been conveyed to a living person, or the required action has been taken.

Miss Hole cites numerous instances of this type of ghost in her fascinating survey, including the story of the female specter whose history was almost completely revealed on the title page of a pamphlet about her published in 1820 and reproduced here!

Q

QUEEN ANNE'S COUNTY GHOST

The ghost that appeared in Queen Anne's County is the subject of a famous American ghost story first related in an excessively rare pamphlet published in the early nineteenth century and bearing the fulsome title: "Authentic Account of the Appearance of a Ghost in Queen Anne's County, Maryland. Proved in Said County Court in the Remarkable Trial, State of Maryland, Use of James, Fanny, Robert and Thomas Harris Versus Mary Harris, Administratrix of James Harris. From Attested Notes Taken in Court at the Time By One of the Council. Baltimore, 1807." In the rather long-winded account, it is reported how the ghost of James Harris returned to torment his eldest daughter, Mary Harris, who was endeavoring to deprive his other children of their rightful share of his estate. It was apparently as a result of his appearances, telling them of their loss, that the four heirs took their elder sister to court and established their claim. Although the pamphlet does not state the outcome of the trial, it is believed that so vividly were the ghost's actions described in court that the judge ruled in favor of the four children. Thereafter, the spirit of James Harris was never seen again.

An illustration from the nineteenth-century American account of the Queen Anne's County Ghost

QUEEN'S HOUSE

The Queen's House at the National Maritime Museum in Greenwich, London is said to be haunted by two figures dressed in the cloaks and cowls of monks. Extraordinary confirmation of this haunting was apparently given in 1966 when a Canadian tourist, the Reverend R. W. Hardy, took a photograph of the beautiful spiral Tulip Staircase in the house and later found on the print two shadowy figures just like monks in the process of climbing the stairs! Reverend Hardy insisted that no one else had been on the staircase at the time, and subsequent investigation of the area has detected the sounds of ghostly footsteps and strange, muttering noises.

QUINNS LIGHT

Quinns Light is a strange, ghostly phenomenon reported in Australia that is actually rather similar to the corpse candle or will-o'-the-wisp of the British Isles. It appears as a phosphorescent light about the size of a large bird, and

The Australian phenomenon known as Quinns Light, which can lure anyone foolish enough to follow it to his or her death

goes round and round in circles before disappearing as mysteriously as it appeared. It is most often reported in the bush areas, and there are numerous eyewitness accounts by people who have pursued Quinns Lights and even fired at them—but to no avail. The Australians also have the Min-Min lights, which appear in cemeteries and seem to dance among the gravestones. This phenomenon is, in all probability, caused by escaping marsh gas.

R

RACETRACK GHOST

The famous Happy Valley Racetrack in Hong Kong has the unique distinction of being haunted by the ghost of a jockey. The haunting originates from 1960 when a jockey named Marcel Samarig, who was beating his horse unmercifully was thrown and killed. Shortly thereafter there were reports of a phantom horse galloping around the track, while the misty form of a jockey, in the same racing colors that Samarig had worn, was seen in the locker rooms. Because other ghosts have also been reported in this vicinity—these spirits apparently having originated from the huge cemeteries on the overlooking hillside—Buddhists have regularly held services of exorcism in order to appease the spirits of the dead.

RADIANT BOY

Impressive Corby Castle in England is haunted by a small, glimmering spirit known as the "Radiant Boy," whose origins are uncertain, although he has been appearing for over two hundred years. In all probability he was a servant in the castle who died under mysterious circumstances. According to Catherine Crowe, who writes about the "beautiful boy" in her *The Night Side of Nature* (1848) he is "clothed in white, with bright locks, resembling gold, and has a mild and benevolent expression."

RAYNHAM HALL

Raynham Hall, a beautiful old country mansion in England, is the home of the brown lady, one of the most famous of English ghosts. The best account of this phantom, garbed in an Elizabethan ruff and brown dress, has been given by Captain Frederick Marryat (1792–1848), the outstanding writer of sea stories, who lived close to Raynham Hall for a number of years. When the owners of the house complained to Marryat about the strange figure who was disturbing their sleep, he offered to sit up with a pistol and apprehend what he believed would prove to be a real-life felon intent on robbery. After two fruitless nights, the brown lady suddenly appeared before him in a hallway "grinning in a malicious and diabolical manner," as he reported in his account of the haunting, *There Is No Death* (1844). Instantly he fired his pistol into the terrifying face and the spirit disappeared. The following morning the bullet was found lodged in the opposite wall of the passageway, and Captain Marryat declared himself convinced the ghost story was true. The gunshot evidently did not deter the brown lady, for she continued to appear over the years, and in September 1936 was actually photographed in Raynham Hall! This occurred in September 1936 while Captain Provand, a professional photographer, was taking pictures of the great oak staircase in the Hall. As he worked, he suddenly caught sight of an ethereal, veiled form descending the stairs, and with great presence of mind snapped off a picture. The resultant photograph, published in *Country Life* magazine of December 26, 1939, has been examined by experts and defied all attempts to prove it faked in any way. Evidence such as this gives the Brown Lady of Raynham Hall a position of preeminence in the history of ghosts.

Fake photograph allegedly showing the young lady's Indian spirit guide

AMERICAN INDIANS

The popular belief that the "spirit guides" of many mediums appear in the form of American Indians has evolved from the fact that the spiritualist movement developed in America, where early mediums claimed their instructions from the "other side" came by way of guides who called themselves "Red Feather" or something equally Indian in origin. The topic is fully discussed in *A Survey of the Occult* (ed., Julian Franklyn, 1935).

RED SEA

The Red Sea is often mentioned in tales of the exorcizing of ghosts, according to Christina Hole in *Haunted England* (1940). Apparently, it became traditional for ghosts to be banished from wherever they were haunting to the Red Sea and there "laid for a thousand years." It has never been very clear, Miss Hole says, as to why they should be conveyed to that remote locality, although "probably the Biblical associations and the sense of immense distance suggested by the name to the average untravelled countryman accounts for the legend." She also relates the story of a Northamptonshire man who said there were no ghosts left in the county because "a deadly long time ago, the paasons all laid their yeads togither and hiked 'em off to the Red Sea."

RELIGIOUS VISIONS

The literature of all religions is full of stories of supernatural apparitions, and this is particularly true of the Christian religion. Perhaps the most

St. Anthony, the founder of Christain monasticism, who was frequently tempted by beautiful ghostly figures

famous account of this kind concerns St. Anthony, whose encounters with ghostly phenomena of one kind and another have been a favorite subject for artists over the years. He was the founder of Christian monasticism, but suffered much temptation in his search for godliness—in particular from a beautiful female ghost who tried to seduce him. The eighteenth-century engraving reproduced here is typical of many pictures illustrating this famous incident. Not surprisingly, a good many religious visions have been reported occurring in churches, just like the accompanying photograph of a ghostly figure snapped in the pulpit at Oberdollendorf Church in Germany by a Mr. H. B. King in 1970. The whole topic is discussed at some length in *Unbidden Guests* by William Oliver Stevens (1949).

REVENANT

Revenant is often thought to be just another word for a ghost, but actually its original meaning was to describe any being that returned from the dead after

The ghostly figure of a priest photographed at Oberdollendorf Church in Germany in 1970

a long absence. Vampires, for example, were believed to be revenants, possessing the power to revive themselves after apparently lying dead for some while. The revenant, in fact, is quite unlike the traditional ghost, for it may well wait years or even centuries before appearing again for the first time. Unlike a vampire too, it does not require human blood to sustain itself. Another distinguishing feature of these spirits is the fact that they are always fully dressed in the garments they wore in life. They are sometimes reported in groups, too, like the band of Ojibwa Indians who were killed in a battle with soldiers over a century ago and have been seen again recently stalking the area where they died, all of them adorned in full war dress. The most famous story of a revenant is that of John Steinlin, who terrorized the diocese of Constance in the seventeenth century and whose story is told in "The Altheim Revenant" included in *The Haunters and the Haunted* by Ernest Rhys (1921).

RINEHART, MARY ROBERTS (1876–1958)

Mrs. Rinehart, author of the famous mystery drama, *The Bat* (1920), was deeply interested in the supernatural, and twice witnessed the activities of poltergeists. The vivid accounts of the spirit that terrorized a household on

A group of revenants as seen by an early nineteenth-century artist

Long Island and another that caused considerable destruction in a Washington apartment that had formerly been occupied by a United States Senator named Boise Penrose are to be found in her autobiography, *My Story* (1931).

RUDRA

Rudra is an Indian god who is said to rule ghosts and evil spirits, and it has been customary for centuries to make offerings to him in order to prevent him sending out his battalions of phantoms to plague the living. Because the Indians believe their ghosts have a habit of gathering at crossroads, they leave their offerings to Rudra at such places. Sir James Frazer discusses this deity in his work, *The Golden Bough* (1890).

RUNNING WATER

A superstition found throughout the world says that no ghost can cross over running water for streams are believed to be holy places—in particular those that run in a southerly direction. In the service of exorcism, holy water is, of course, used to rid any haunted place of a troublesome phantom, and this will be most effective if it has been drawn from a clear, fast-running brook.

S

SAGE LEAVES

Superstition credits sage leaves with the power to enable people to see ghosts. According to an old English tradition, if a young girl goes out into the garden on Halloween night at midnight and picks twelve sage leaves, and then waits quietly, the shadowy figure of her future husband will materialize in the gloom. In Lancashire it is said the same thing will happen if the young woman walks around the local churchyard twelve times on the same day and at the same hour.

ST. ELMO'S FIRE

St. Elmo's Fire is ghostly lights that appear on ships at sea, and it has been reported by sailors for centuries. These eerie lights attach themselves to the masts and make a crackling sound. If one falls to the deck and begins to glow around a particular seaman, this is said to be a sign that the man is shortly going to die. According to an old legend, St. Elmo was the patron saint of Mediterranean sailors. He died while at sea during a storm, but promised the crew before his death that if they were not fated to die like him, he would get a message back to them. When, a short while later, a glowing light like a candle flame appeared on the mast, the sailors believed Elmo had sent his message. Ever since it has been claimed that the appearance of St. Elmo's Fire signifies the worst of a storm is over. What in fact happens is that the light is caused by electrical discharges as the weather begins to clear!

SAMPFORD GHOST

The poltergeist that haunted the family of Mr. John Chave at Sampford Peverell in Devon, England, is now recognized as one of the classic ghost stories, and the events were recorded in a most fulsome account kept at the time by the Reverend Caleb Colton, and later published as *The Narrative of the Sampford Ghost*, (1810). For three years from 1807, Mr. Chave, his family and servants were plagued by the ghost who filled the house with terrible crashes and bangs during both the day and night. Invisible hands also attacked some of the occupants, and various small objects were seen flying about the rooms. Like virtually every other poltergeist case on record, the haunting ceased as suddenly and mysteriously as it had begun, and the march of time has been unable to provide any clear explanation as to the cause—although the later discovery of secret passageways in the house and the knowledge that smugglers were active at the time has led to the suggestion that the whole affair may have been a fraud.

SCOTT, SIR WALTER (1771-1832)

Sir Walter Scott, who is widely considered one of the world's greatest historical novelists, was deeply interested in the supernatural and wrote several classic short ghost stories including "Wandering Willie's Tale" and "The Tapestried Chamber." Sir Walter himself had a brush with the unknown, hearing strange scratching noises in his home, Abbotsford in Roxburghshire. Although he saw nothing, the great novelist came to believe the house was haunted and this reputation has clung to the building over the intervening years.

SCREAMING SKULLS

There are a number of very bizarre stories to be found in ghost history concerning human skulls that have made the most hideous screaming noises whenever any attempts were made to move them from their last resting places. In each case it is claimed that the owner of the skull had left specific instructions about what was to happen to his or her body after death and, when these wishes were ignored, used the skull as the medium for carrying out the most terrifying hauntings. The best known of these screaming skulls is the one still preserved at Bettiscombe Manor in England, (*see* illustration), which belonged to a black slave who told his master that if his body was not returned to the West Indies after his death, he would curse the place. The owner apparently took no notice of the threat and ever since then the ancient, yellowing skull has extracted vengeance by defying all attempts to move it—including burial—by making such alarming disturbances that the occupiers have been forced to put it back in the old bureau where it has lain for over two hundred years. Christina Hole devotes a whole chapter in her book, *Haunted England* (1940) to screaming skulls, and apart from the example at Bettiscombe Manor also cites other troublesome skulls at Higher Chilton in Somerset, Wardley Hall, Manchester, Warbleton Prior in Sussex, Calgarth House on Lake Windermere, and another famous instance at Burton Agnes Hall in Yorkshire.

SEANCE

A seance is a gathering normally staged under the auspices of practicing spiritualists at which a medium—a person who claims to be able to make contact with the spirit world—endeavors to produce either physical phenomena (the likenesses of human beings composed of ectoplasm) or mental phenomena (the voices of dead people). This ability is said to be inherent, and

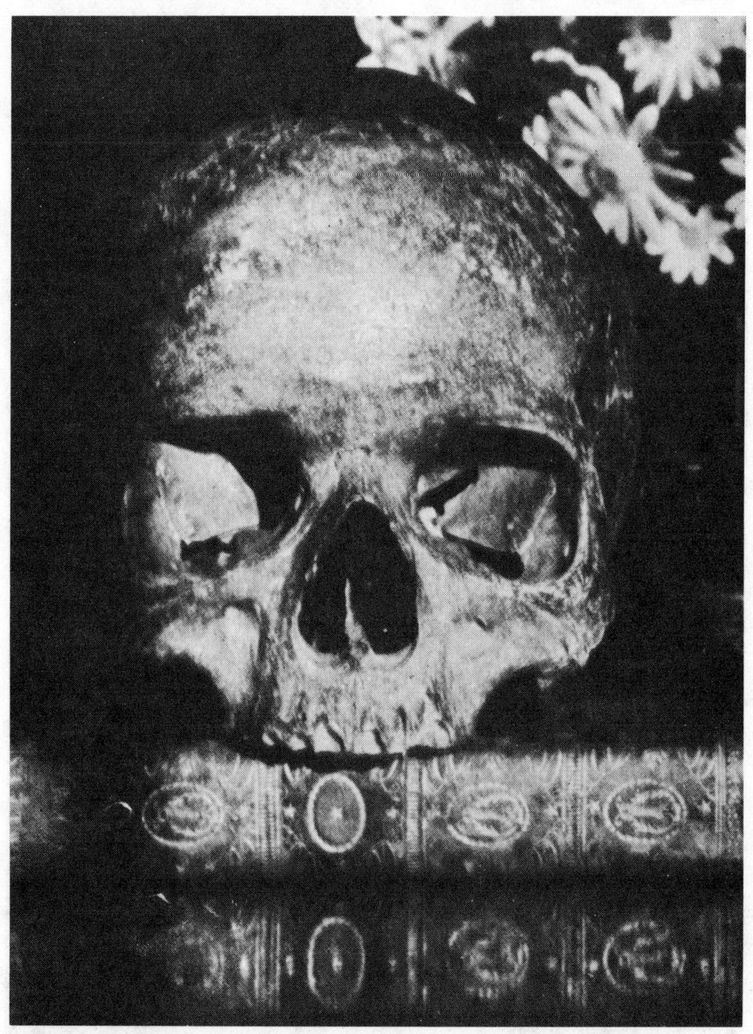

The famous Screaming Skull of Bettiscombe Manor in England, which causes disturbances whenever it is moved from the house

at its most highly developed is claimed to be powerful enough to cause materializations of spirits. The word seance is from the French and means "a sitting," and at these gatherings it is customary for two, four, six or eight people to sit in a circle, linking their hands together with those of the medium. The medium then goes into a trance, during which the phenomena are said to appear, usually preceded by a dramatic change in the temperature of the room where the seance is being held. There are innumerable reports of materializations taking place at seances, but perhaps the most remarkable on record were those conducted during the 1960s by the American medium Ethel Post-Parrish of Pennsylvania. Mrs. Post-Parrish materialized an Indian girl whom she called "Silver Belle," and on one notable occasion produced this spirit before an audience of eighty people. The photographs on page 170 and

171 were taken during this seance by use of an infrared film. An interesting work on this subject is *Clairvoyance and Materialisation* by Dr. Gustave Gely (1927).

SEER OF POUGHKEEPSIE

Andrew Jackson Davis (1826–88), who was called the "Seer of Poughkeepsie," is credited with having "laid the foundation stone of Spiritualism" according to Lionel A. Weatherly in his *The Supernatural* (1891). Davis, a poorly educated shoemaker who was born in Poughkeepsie, New York, went

Three photographs from a remarkable sequence taken at a seance conducted by Ethel Post-Parrish, showing her Indian spirit guide, "Silver Belle" materializing

through a number of "ecstatic" periods during which he gained an insight into the "unseen world" and as a result in 1847 published a work grandiosely entitled *The Principles of Nature, Her Divine Revelations and A Voice to Mankind.* He claimed to have dictated the book over a period of fifteen months while in a series of hypnotic trances, and that the information had been given to him by discarnate spirits. Commenting on the work in *A Survey of the Occult* (ed., Julian Franklyn, 1935), S. G. Soal says, "As a contribution to the scientific knowledge of his day, Davis's work was of negligible value and is indeed full of absurdities. Yet it possessed a sort of crude imaginative power, which caused it to become an instant best seller, and its author to be proclaimed the herald of a new religious era." It was not long after the publication of this book that the Fox sisters in Hydesville heard the knocking sounds in their home, which led directly to the founding of the spiritualist movement.

SHAKESPEARE, WILLIAM (1564–1616)

The supernatural was perhaps more widely employed in English drama during Elizabethan times than at any other period, and much of the credit for this is due to William Shakespeare, who was, of course, deeply interested in all aspects of the topic, and ghosts in particular. He, perhaps more than any other dramatist, realized the problems in trying to present something as ethereal as a ghost on the stage, as S. G. Soal has written in *A Survey of the Occult* (ed., Julian Franklyn, 1935):

> Shakespeare clearly realised that ghosts and witches could not of themselves guarantee the highest imaginative effect. To achieve this, he saw, it was

One of several incidents in William Shakespeare's plays that underlines his interset in ghosts and the supernatural

> essential to show a sensitive mind reacting to their power of suggestion, and the finer the mind the richer would be the effect. Moreover, like all great dramatists, he suggests the presence of supernatural forces without necessarily introducing the spectral. The working of fate, the use of tragic irony, and the description of such perturbations of nature as accompanied the murder of Caesar and Duncan are among the means whereby he endows human action with more than human significance.

His plays *Julius Caesar* and *Macbeth* with their powerful ghost scenes are, of course, too well known to need description here, and in both instances it is Caesar's ghost in the one and Banquo's ghost in the other that somehow dominate the entire action. In *Hamlet,* too, there are some memorable ghostly moments and Shakespeare also shows us how the supernatural may be used in comedy in both *A Midsummer Night's Dream* and *The Tempest.* The subject of Shakespeare and his involvement with, and interest in, the supernatural beliefs of his times has been dealt with at length in many studies, in particular in Dover Wilson's *Life in Shakespeare's England* (1911).

SHINS

Apart from being the most populous nation on earth, China also had more ghosts than any other nation—its tradition listing no fewer than sixty different kinds of shins, or evil ghosts. Each of these has a specific day for appearing during a cycle of sixty days that is endlessly repeated. To appease these ghosts the Chinese leave outside their houses small gifts of cakes that bear a message addressed to the "honorable homeless ghosts" begging them to enjoy the gift and then depart from the property in peace. Catching sight of one of these phantoms can be an unnerving experience, for they first appear as a shapeless mist, gradually forming into the shape of a human, with the head materializing first, then the feet, and finally the body in between! That is not their only peculiarity—for Chinese ghosts have no chins!

SHIP O' THE DEAD

An old tradition widely recorded maintains that whenever an old sailor—in particular a pirate—dies on land and not at sea, a phantom ship known as the "Ship o' the Dead" comes sailing in through the air from the ocean to fetch his ghost. According to *A Survey of the Occult* (1935), in which this topic is discussed, in Borneo the ship is shaped like a bird and actually takes the souls of *all* sea-faring men.

SHIPWRECKS

There is a superstition among sailors never to cross directly over any area of sea where a ship has been wrecked or sunk as this is likely to disturb the spirits

A magic lantern slide of a "Ship o' the Dead" coming to fetch the ghost of an old sailor who has just died

of the seamen who were drowned there and as a result they will then come and haunt the boat and its crew.

SHOCK

The shock is a ghost, peculiar to the English county of Suffolk, which looks rather like a dog or small donkey and has a shaggy mane and saucer eyes. There are several stories of shocks in the anonymous volume *Country Folk Lore* (1900).

SHOJO

According to Japanese legend, the oceans are populated with sea ghosts known as shojo, who have vivid red hair but intend no harm to sailors. They are apparently addicted to drinking and making merry, and when seen are usually dancing on the waves. Because their favorite drink is sake, one tradition says it is possible to catch a shojo by luring it onto land with a jar of the drink.

SHRIEKING PITS, THE

At Aylmerton in England are a number of large, circular pits that are thought to have been the remains of a prehistoric settlement. Over the years they have become known as the "Shrieking Pits" because of a white figure that is said to haunt them and that occasionally emits the most terrible and agonizing cries. Despite the persistence of the stories, folklorist Christina Hole in her *Haunted England* (1940) believes that this is one haunting that could be explained by natural rather than supernatural causes—the effects being created by a mixture of mist and bird noises.

SILKY

The silky is a female ghost who wears rustling silk clothing and does domestic chores in the house after the family has gone to bed. Silkies are particularly found near the border between England and Scotland and are said to terrorize lazy servants and people who do not do their work. The most famous of these ghosts was the Silky of Black Heddon, who is referred to in William Henderson's *Folk-Lore of the Northern Counties* (1879). Another silky that haunted an area of North Shields was believed to have been the ghost of a mistress of the Duke of Argyll, who was murdered by her lover during the reign of William III.

SIN-EATER

The sin-eater is a term to describe an old-established custom, found predominantly in Wales, in which a person is paid to take upon himself the sins of a newly dead person so that that person's soul is free to leave the body and go to heaven, instead of remaining earthbound and becoming a ghost. The sin-eater places small dishes containing salt and bread on the chest of the corpse, and then ceremonially eats them. By doing so he not only "takes on" the departed person's sins, but also earns himself a substantial fee. As a matter of interest, salt has long been considered a defense against evil spirits.

A contemporary engraving of the highly dangerous Smithfield Market Ghost, which attacked butchers during the middle years of the seventeenth century

SMITHFIELD MARKET GHOST

The ghost that haunted Smithfield meat market in England in the middle of the seventeenth century is one of the most curious on record—as well as seemingly being one of the most dangerous. A pamphlet published in 1654 called *A True Relation of the Smithfield Ghost,* complete with the accompanying illustration, describes the phantom as dressed in the gown of a lawyer, with horns on his head, a meat cleaver in his hand, and long, pointed shoes on his feet! The spirit apparently appeared every Saturday night between nine o'clock and midnight and plagued the butchers by pulling joints of meat off their stalls. Although some of these men bravely attempted to drive the figure off with their own cleavers and chopping knives, "they cannot feel anything but aire" according to the pamphlet. The description of the ghost being in lawyer's garb was the giveaway, because apparently a local lawyer named Mallet had died just prior to the outbreak from eating poisoned meat! Mallet was said to be unsure who had sold the meat, however, because after terrorizing Smithfield he moved on "unto Whitechappell and Eastcheape and did even more mischief to the butchers than ever Robin Goodfellow did to Country Hides." The ghost eventually disappeared as suddenly as it had appeared, and the mystery has remained as to whether he was a genuine phantom or merely a clever prankster.

SMOKE GHOSTS

The curious phenomenon of smoke ghosts has been reported in both Europe and America for many years, a famous story being that of a girl in the United States who was burned to death during the seventeenth century and whose ghostly presence has ever since been recognizable by its accompanying pungent odor of smoke. In 1954 the most peculiar of this type of ghost was reported in the Tower of London. A sentry suddenly noticed a smoke cloud that moved of its own volition, changed its shape, and did not seem to diffuse or drift like ordinary smoke. After watching it for some minutes, the man set off in pursuit—but at this the smoke disappeared instantly. Further details of this phenomenon are to be found in *Ghosts and Hauntings* by Dennis Bardens (1967).

SPECTER

Specter is another word generally thought to mean just a ghost or apparition, but among ghost-hunters and specialists in psychic phenomena it has become employed to describe hauntings that subsequently *prove* to be explainable or deliberately fraudulent. The most famous of such examples is probably the Specter of the Brocken from Germany, which is detailed under its own entry in this dictionary. The specter monk reproduced on page 178 is typical of the fraudulent photographs of this type of ghost produced for gullible Victorians

A smoke ghost as shown in an old engraving, *circa* 1838

during the closing years of the last century. It was the handiwork of a London photographer named W. Dean. The word specter derives from the Latin *spectrum*, a vision, and the whole topic is discussed by C. J. S. Thompson in his *History of Ghosts and Hauntings* (1930).

SPECTER OF THE BROCKEN

The Specter of the Brocken Mountain has for generations been one of the most famous ghost stories to be heard in Germany—and indeed for a long time many people went in fear of climbing the mountain in case they came

An effective but nonetheless fraudulent photograph entitled "The Specter Monk"

face to face with the great towering figure of the specter. The Brocken, which is over 3,300 feet high and, as such, is one of the tallest mountains in the Harz Range, had long been regarded with unease for it was traditionally believed to be a meeting point for witches and demons—these evil-doers meeting regularly on the mountain top to conduct their terrible revels. Then, when reports began to be made about an awesome ghostly figure that loomed up out of the mist upon unwary travellers, the place seemed doubly terrifying.

Two German travelers discovering how their shadows cast on the clouds create the Specter of the Brocken

However, in 1818, the Specter of the Brocken was "laid" by a German scholar named Gustav Jordan. Several times he visited the Brocken in search of the specter—and on each occasion caught a glimpse of it. Then one day the secret of the mystery suddenly dawned upon him. It was all a trick of the light! He wrote in his *Journal* of March 1818:

> Having thus had an opportunity of discovering the whole secret of this phenomenon, I can give the following information to such of my readers as may be desirous of seeing it themselves. When the rising sun, and, according to analogy, the case will be the same at the setting sun, throws his rays over the Brocken upon the body of a man standing opposite to fine light clouds, floating around or hovering past him, he needs only fix his eyes steadfastly upon them, and, in all probability, he will see the singular spectacle of his own shadow extending the length of five or six hundred feet, at the distance of about two miles before him. This is one of the most agreeable phenomena I ever had an opportunity of remarking on the great observatory of Germany.

Despite this explanation, the legend of the Specter of the Brocken still persists in Germany today and attracts many tourists to the Harz Mountains.

SPIRIT LIGHTS

Numerous mediums have produced luminous phenomena known as "spirit lights" either by fraud or supernormal means, according to S. G. Soal in *A Survey of the Occult* (1935), who quotes from personal experience. "Phosphorescent lights were seen by the writer at seances of the American medium, Amy Burton, who visited England under the pseudonym Ada Bessinet in 1921," he writes. "The lights appeared suddenly in the darkness in quick

The luminous phenomena known as "Spirit Lights." This photograph was produced by a South American medium named Madame Olivia

succession, rising and disappearing." Professor Soal was unable to detect any fraud on this occasion, but says it is possible for such lights to be produced in a darkened room by using either glass balls filled with phosphorus oil or by rubbing ferro-cerium on the fingers. The spirit lights produced by the South American medium Madame Olivia (photographed here) were among the most spectacular of any recorded—bluish-white flashes that darted around the sitters at her seances.

SPIRIT PHOTOGRAPHS

Like many of the other phenomena associated with spiritualism, spirit photography—photographs allegedly showing a person still alive complete with the head and shoulders of a deceased relative hovering above them—originated in America in the middle of the last century. A man named

A typical example of a spirit photograph taken during the Victorian era

William Mumler of Boston is credited with having produced the first such pictures in 1862, and from his humble (and fraudulent) beginnings a whole style of photography blossomed on both sides of the Atlantic. Almost without exception the spirit figures were introduced onto the photographic plates by double exposure and the liberal use of cotton wool to give a suitably misty effect. Several of the more famous spirit photographers are represented in this book, along with examples of their work, and all of them undoubtedly deserve the observation of S. G. Soal in *A Survey of the Occult* (1935): "There is perhaps no phase of mediumship to which spiritualists cling more tenaciously than the alleged appearance, on photographic plates, of the faces of deceased persons, and we may add that for no class of phenomena is the evidence more contemptible." Predictably spirit photographers became rarer as the public learned about the tricks the camera was capable of, and the last of the successful fakers, a man named John Myers, was not able to continue beyond the middle 1930s. As Simeon Edmunds has written in *"Spirit" Photography* (1968): "Every spirit photographer who has been thoroughly and competently investigated has been proved fraudulent. No reliable record appears to exist of a definitely recognized spirit extra being obtained on any photograph under completely fraud-proof conditions." Perhaps the most interesting, though unfortunately the most biased, study of the subject is *The Case for Spirit Photography* by Sir Arthur Conan Doyle (1922), who was himself photographed in this manner on several occasions.

SPIRITUALISM

Spiritualism is a world-wide belief that believes that a person's spirit survives after death, and that it is possible to make contact with this spirit through the intermediary of a medium at a seance. The subject is dealt with comprehensively in numerous studies, in particular by Maurice Barbanell in his *Spiritualism Today* (1969).

SPOKEVELD

The Spokeveld, or "spooky country," is a famous area of haunted countryside in South Africa on the southern edge of the Great Karoo between the Patatas River and the Southkloff. It is a bleak and desolate area that is popularly believed to be the haunt of ghosts and demons. Also, according to Eric Rosenthal in his book *They Walk By Night* (1949), "the most frequently seen is a spectral wagon which, with phantom drivers, rushes furiously across the veld in the still hours of the morning just preceding daybreak." Phantom coaches have also been reported in South Africa on the Port Elizabeth highway, on the suitably named Hex River Mountains and in the Drakensberg where, apart from coaches, a phantom motor car has also been sighted!

SPOOK

The spook is a type of ghost only found in America and it is said to be a benevolent rather than a harmful spirit. The first legends of spooks are found among the traditions of the American Indians, who believed that these spirits could take over control of the body of a living person. The ghosts can apparently haunt a person without him or her being aware of it, absorbing themselves into that person whenever they so desire. Among the rural people of several Eastern states there are stories of men whose lives were failures until their spook took them over and enabled them to achieve wealth and position. The word "spook" is now, of course, also much used to describe private spies and government surveillance agencies.

SPOOKLAND

An enormously successful book entitled *Raymond, or Life and Death* published in 1916 by Sir Oliver Lodge (1851–1940), the distinguished physicist, purports to give a picture of what the life of ghosts is actually like. This extraordinary work was based on conversations Sir Oliver said he had with his son Raymond, who had been killed earlier during the First World War, and were made possible through a medium named Mrs. Gladys Leonard. In Spookland, said Raymond Lodge, spirits live in houses made of bricks and surrounded by trees and flowers. They have bodies that appear to them as substantial as ours do to us. They see the sun as we do, and the earth on which they live is so real that when he knelt down, Raymond found his clothes muddied. These clothes were apparently made out of the smells and emanations that arise from terrestrial wardrobes! Although there was much in the book that was farcical—the ghosts still liked their aclohol and smoked cigars, for instance—there is no doubt its popularity had much to do with the emotional times in which it appeared—with thousands being killed in the war and their grieving relatives desperate for any hint that there might be an afterlife.

SPUNKIES

An old tradition says that spunkies are particularly sad ghosts, being the spirits of unbaptized children. They are found both on land and at sea—wandering about country lanes looking for someone to give them a name, or else luring unsuspecting ships to their doom. In Scotland it is said that spunkies sometimes gather together to assuage their loneliness, while in Western England they have the power to turn themselves into small white moths and go about unnoticed among human beings. According to Ruth Tongue in her book *Country Folklore* (1970), spunkies are doomed to wander until Judgment Day, but every Halloween they go to church to meet the spirits of those who have recently died.

STONE AGE GHOST

Perhaps the oldest ghost recorded anywhere in the world is that of the Stone Age man who gallops on horseback across Cranborne Chase in England. This strange phantom clad in fur skins rides his shaggy mount without bridle or stirrups and brandishes what looks like a stone axe in his hand. The Stone Age ghost is usually seen in the vicinity of Dorset, and this has led to the suggestion that he is the soul of a warrior who once dwelt in that area.

SUMMERS, MONTAGUE (1880–1948)

Montague Summers, who claimed to be a Roman Catholic priest, was an expert on witchcraft, vampires, werewolves and demonology, and wrote books on all these subjects that are now considered classics of their kind, albeit rather narrow in their viewpoints and occasionally incredibly naive. Summers was also deeply interested in ghost lore, and edited two fine collections of ghost stories, *The Supernatural Omnibus* (1931) and *Victorian Ghost Stories* (1933), which are models of their kind. He also claimed to have seen a ghost himself while visiting in the country—that of a hunchbacked, pale-faced girl who wandered the rooms of the family home where she had lived out her unhappy life until she committed suicide in the middle years of the nineteenth century.

T

TABLE-TURNING

In the year 1853 a craze for table-turning developed in England and France. It was claimed that when a group of people gathered around a table with their hands upon it, spirits of the dead would pass on messages by the manner in which the piece of furniture tilted. S. G. Soal explains about this craze in *A Survey of the Occult* (1935):

> It was found that when four or five persons stood around a light circular table with their hands resting upon it, the table would tilt and sometimes rotate. The sense of the rotation conformed to the general expectation of the people standing around. If one half of the sitters expected it to rotate in a clockwise sense, and the other half counterclockwise, the table would remain at rest. The great physicist Michael Faraday (1791–1867) showed by means of ingenious experiments that the movement of the table was caused by the unconscious muscular pressure of the hands resting on it. What Faraday did not explain, however, was why the table should tilt out (by the use of the alphabet) messages which were often quite unexpected by any of the people present.

The subject is discussed in further detail in Mr. Soal's essay.

TAKARABUNE

The *Takarabune* is the phantom treasure ship of the Japanese that is supposed to sail into port on New Year's Day bringing good fortune to all who see it. According to a tradition still observed, if a picture of this ghostly vessel is purchased on New Year's Day and placed under the pillow, it will ensure a year of good luck for the sleeper.

TALKING MONGOOSE

The case of "Gef," the talking mongoose of the Isle of Man, is widely held to be the most extraordinary animal ghost story of this century—and it is certainly one of the best known. In the autumn of 1936, strange noises were reported at an old farmhouse known as Cashens Gap, at Dalby, England. Soon the owner of the house, a Mr. Irving, reported seeing a shadow moving about the rooms of the farmhouse, and then tiny furry feet were spotted through a crack in the ceiling. Most extraordinary of all, the creature began to *talk* to Mr. Irving, identifying itself as "Gef," a mongoose! Subsequently, the haunting and the house were investigated by journalists as well as psychic researchers, and none was able to prove it was all a hoax. After the initial blaze of publicity, interest in the talking mongoose—the first recorded instance of a ghostly animal able to communicate with human beings—declined somewhat, and even "Gef" made his presence felt less and less frequently. Some years afterwards, a later owner of the farmhouse reported shooting a small furry creature in the grounds of Cashens Gap, but whether this was the talking mongoose has never been satisfactorily established. The full story of this phenomenon is recounted in admirable detail in *The Haunting of Cashens Gap* by Harry Price and R. S. Lambert (1936).

TANWEDD

The tanwedd is an eerie spherical light that appears over the homes of Welsh families. If it remains stationary, a member of that family will be taken ill shortly or meet with an accident. However, if it actually descends on the house, then one or more members of the family will die within the next few days.

TASH

A tash or thevshi is the Irish word for a ghost and, such spirits can appear in human or animal form; indeed the country is particularly noted for the number of legends about phantom dogs, cats, horses (headless and otherwise), birds, rabbits and even insects such as butterflies—not forgetting the famous banshee and phouka, of course. Quite a large percentage of these ghosts are said to be the spirits of people who died violent deaths, either having been murdered or having committed suicide, and the Irish believe such souls are condemned to bring attention to themselves and their folly by haunting the place where they died as a lesson to others. In many country districts it is still held to be unwise to mourn for anyone for too long "or else they will be kept from their rest and return as a ghost." Ireland has a strong ghost-story tradition and gave birth to perhaps the greatest of all ghost-story writers, Joseph Sheridan Le Fanu (1814–73). Many stories of Irish hauntings ranging from "The Headless Rider of Castle Sheela" and "The Bloody Stones of Kerrigan's Keep" to "The Winged Dagger of Braghee" and "The Shriek of Slaney" are to be found in James Reynolds's two spendid collections, *Ghosts in Irish Houses* (1947) and *More Ghosts in Irish Houses* (1956).

TASMANIA

According to Joyce Zwarycz in her book *Visits From Beyond The Grave* (1975), no state in Australia can boast as many ghosts as Tasmania "where they range from spectres of humans, headless and otherwise, to phantom horses and dogs, haunted wells and even spirit-world carriages complete with beautiful women ghosts in crinolines." However, Mrs. Zwarycz believes the

Another of the Irish spirits, the tash, can appear in either human or animal shape

strangest of these stories concerns a stone building known as Garth that stands on the bank of the South Esk, a few miles from Fingal. It was built by a young English settler in readiness for his prospective bride coming out to join him. "So anxious was the young man," the authoress says, "to bring the young lady to Australia that he sailed for London before the house was completed. But on arrival in England he found he had been jilted, so he returned all the way to Garth where he hanged himself in the courtyard of the unfinished building. His ghost, they say, still haunts the place." Mrs. Zwarycz says that the building is also haunted by the ghost of a woman and child—the child having jumped into a well for fear of the woman, who also drowned in attempting to rescue the infant. The authoress adds, "Today this sinister old house stands abandoned. The upstairs rooms and the hall are still unfinished just as the workmen left them."

THEATER GHOSTS

The Man in Gray is London's best-known theater ghost and he has been reported on numerous occasions in the famous Theatre Royal in Drury Lane. His story is told by theater historian W. Macqueen-Pope in his book *Theatre Royal, Drury Lane,* who describes him as a man in a white wig, with a three-cornered hat, wearing a gray cloak over his shoulder and riding boots on his feet. He is evidently a man of style and some eyewitnesses say he has a sword. Mr. Pope has seen the ghost himself, and says that he invariably appears between the hours of 9 A.M. and 6 P.M.—before the curtain call of the evening performance, in fact. According to the legend, the Man in Gray was a wealthy young eighteenth-century buck who fell in love with one of the young actresses. In a jealous rage, the girl's current lover murdered the man and secretly hid his body somewhere behind the walls in the theater. Despite this tragic history, the ghost is now regarded with some affection by the actors at the Theatre Royal, for it is believed that if he appears just before the opening of a new production then it is sure of success. Indeed, his presence was particularly noted before the opening of such enormously successful recent musicals as *The Dancing Years, Oklahoma, South Pacific, The King and I* and many more. Among other London theaters that are said to be haunted are the Duke of York's Theatre in St. Martin's Lane (by Victoria Melhotte, the wife of the first owner), the Adelphi in the Strand (by the ghost of the murdered Victorian actor William Ferriss), and the Theatre Royal in the Haymarket (the apparition being that of John Buckstone, a well-known manager-actor).

TOKOLOSH

The tokolosh is South Africa's most famous type of spirit—a strange, semi-human creature who is supposed to live in rivers and other water courses. This is a description of him as given by Mrs. Minnie Martin in Eric Rosenthal's *They Walk By Night* (1949): "He is not much bigger than a baboon, but is minus the tail, and is perfectly black with a quantity of black hair on his body. He has hands and feet like an ordinary mortal, but is never heard to speak. He shuns the daylight . . . and his deeds are cruel, revengeful, apparently unlimited." The tokolosh can also become invisible, and there is a similarity in many of his actions to that of the European poltergeist. Mr. Rosenthal devotes a fascinating chapter to this strange being in his book.

TOLAETH

The tolaeth are strange, ghostly sounds that serve as omens of death in old Welsh families. According to Elliot O'Donnell in *Family Ghosts and Ghostly Phenomena* (1933):

> The Tolaeth are audible phenomena that vary a great deal. Sometimes they are rappings and knockings on the doors or walls of the house in which the doomed person or members of his or her family are living; sometimes ghostly footsteps that tramp up and down staircases and along passages, invariably halting outside the door of the doomed person; and sometimes rumbling sounds, like the wheels of a heavy vehicle, that stops outside the house of the person who is doomed to die shortly.

TOMMY RAWHEAD

Tommy Rawhead is a ghost found in the English countryside who preys on children, attempting to lure them into quagmires or dangerous ponds where they will drown, and he can then claim their souls. There is a report about Tommy by Samuel Johnson in his famous *Dictionary* (1747–55) in which he defines him as "The name of a spectre, mentioned to frighten children" and he also cites two other accounts by John Dryden and John Locke. In Lancashire and Yorkshire it is still common to hear parents chide their youngsters with the words, "Keep away from the marl-pit or Rawhead will have you!"

TOWER OF LONDON

The Tower of London has been called "the most haunted place on earth," which considering the number of people who have been executed or died there during its 900 years of existence is perhaps not surprising! The best-known ghost is that of Anne Boleyn, one of Henry VIII's wives, who was beheaded on Tower Green and now wanders the area with her head underneath her arm. The Bloody Tower is also said to be haunted by several phantoms of men who were executed there, while a strange, blue-white specter has been reported more than once in the Crown Jewels House.

TREES

The belief that certain trees are haunted is a very ancient tradition, and in his book devoted to the subject, *Trees of Ghostly Dread* (1958) Elliott O'Donnell writes,

> To the mind that is at all imaginative there is often something very ghostly in the appearance of trees in the dusk; their fantastically fashioned, knotted and gnarled branches can bear such an unpleasant resemblance to bony arms with long, curved fingers outstretched, as if in readiness to pounce on one. The rustling of the leaves as a breeze stirs them sounds like whispering

voices, and the singing and moaning of the wind like the crying and wailing of lost souls.

In his book, O'Donnell cites numerous world-wide reports of haunted trees including the Fatal Cherry Tree in Canada, the Haunted Navity Wood near Cromarty, Scotland, the Screaming Phantom of Mannheim Forest in Germany, and the Sinister Danmark Tree of the North of England.

TRICKSTER SPIRIT

The beautiful but treacherous Florida Everglades are said to be haunted by a number of "trickster spirits." These are eerie phantoms that appear as misty shapes or dancing lights and can lead the unwary follower to his death in the swamplands. These ghosts are said to be the spirits of Indians who were killed during the Seminole Indian Wars in 1858 and have devoted themselves ever since to revenging themselves on the white man. The "trickster spirit" has, of course, been immortalized in the famous stories of Brer Rabbit written by Joel Chandler Harris (1848–1908).

TURN OF THE SCREW, THE

The Turn of the Screw by Henry James, published in 1898, is justifiably regarded as a classic ghost story and tells with marvellous skill and atmos-

Paperback edition of one of the greatest of all ghost novels, *The Turn of the Screw*, by Henry James, rarely out of print in almost one hundred years

phere how a pair of small children are possessed by the evil spirits of two dead servants. James (1843–1916) was born in America, spent much of his life in Europe, and became a naturalized British citizen just before his death. Apart from his numerous highly successful novels about Anglo-American attitudes, he also wrote a number of short supernatural stories that were all collected together into one volume entitled *The Ghostly Tales of Henry James,* published in 1948.

TURPIN, DICK

The legendary highwayman Dick Turpin is said to gallop in ghostly shape over half the length of Britain—in particular on the roads between London and York. However, the most curious supernatural legend concerning him is focused on the town of Loughton in Essex, where it was said Turpin tortured an old women by holding her over a fire to learn from her where she kept her money hidden. Ever since his death, says the legend, Turpin has been seen riding Black Bess up Trapps Hill in Loughton, with the shape of an old woman clinging to his back. This story is the only recorded example of one ghost being tormented by another! Turpin's ghost has also been seen on Watling Street, between Nuneaton and Hinckley, where he is said to have carried out several daring and brutal robberies. The most recent sighting was in 1968 when a motorist described how a figure on horseback wearing a coat with red sleeves and a three-cornered hat passed him riding on some common land beside the road.

TYRONE GHOST

The Irish legend of the Tyrone Ghost who appeared to Lady Beresford in 1693 is unique in the annals of supernatural lore because the spirit left a memento of his visit by signing his name in a notebook! The ghost was that of Lord Tyrone, who made a pact with his dear friend, Lady Beresford, that whosoever should die first would make every effort to return and confront the other. According to a manuscript account written by Lady Elizabeth Cobb, granddaughter of Lady Beresford, Lord Tyrone did indeed return bearing news of his lady-love's future life, which later proved uncannily accurate. And to prove that it was indeed he, the ghost of Lord Tyrone wrote his easily recognizable signature in her pocket book. He is also said to have touched Lady Beresford's arm with a hand "as cold as marble" and this left her wrist withered for the rest of her life.

U

UFO GHOSTS

Unidentified flying objects—or "flying saucers" as they are more popularly known—have been the subject of endless debate and discussion as to their likelihood and possible source of origin. Apart from the many cases that can be put down to tricks of the light, strange cloud formations and even perfectly natural objects like weather balloons or aircraft, perhaps the strangest suggestion of all is that they are spirit forms, strange materializations not unlike the traditional idea of ghosts, and created from the latent energy of machinery. The theory has been discussed in such books as *The Dragon and the Disc* by F. W. Holiday (1973) and *The UFO Experience* by J. Allen Hynek (1972).

UJEST ARMY

Of all the stories of phantom armies being seen in the sky, the account of the Ujest Army in Silesia in 1785 is perhaps the one that had most eyewitnesses. According to contemporary records, the strange phenomenon occurred in the April of that year during the magnificent funeral being staged for the Silesian military hero, General von Cosel. As the General's coffin was slowly being paraded to the church at Ujest, mourners suddenly noticed a whole line of figures in military uniforms seemingly parading among the clouds.

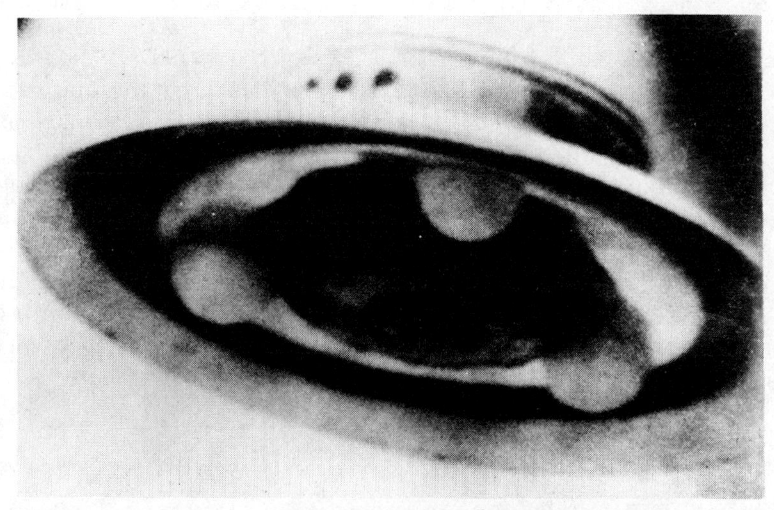

The theory has been advanced that unidentified flying objects—or "flying saucers"—might be a kind of spirit form

Hundreds of people are said to have witnessed the troop of men who were dressed in uniforms of the same period—giving rise to the belief that they were the ghosts of soldiers who died during the General's campaigns, and had assembled once more to honor their commander. An interesting postscript to this account is that several weeks after the funeral the phantom army of Ujest was seen again in the skies—and this time the spirit of General von Cosel was seen at the head of his men!

UMI BOZU

The umi bozu is a giant sea phantom who appears to terrify Japanese seamen, according to a very ancient tradition. This awesome phantom is black in color, has a shaved head and huge staring eyes, and its name means a sea priest or monk.

UNDINE

The undine, or ondine as it is sometimes called, is a beautiful, ghostly female spirit that haunts stretches of water in many European countries. The ghosts are said to be those of young women who died by drowning, usually having committed suicide as a result of a broken love affair, and although they are tragic figures they mean no harm to anyone except heartless lovers. They have been celebrated in a number of poems and stories, and one particularly beautiful and sad creature features in an anonymous German romance called *The Undine,* published in 1846.

UNKNOWN SOLDIER

According to Jack Hallam in his book *The Ghost Tour* (1967), Westminster Abbey in London is haunted by the ghost of a soldier. "Near the tomb of the Unknown Warrior," he writes, "has been seen the ghost of a khaki-clad soldier of World War I, mud-stained and bare-headed. 'His eyes are full of a strange pleading. Always he walks with one hand outstretched as though beseeching someone to do something' said one woman, the mother of three sons killed in the war, who has seen what has become known as the 'Ghost of the Unknown Soldier.' " The abbey also boasts two other ghosts: Father Benedictus, a tall, thin figure in a monk's habit who is believed to have been killed during the reign of Henry VIII, and John Bradshaw, the president of the High Court of Justice, which tried and condemned King Charles I.

UTUKKU

The Utukku was the name given by the ancient Assyrians to the ghost of evil intentions that lay in wait for unsuspecting travellers and could cause anyone they encountered to fall ill soon afterwards. Records indicate that the Assyrians were among the earliest people to take ghosts seriously, and apart from the utukku, had names for two other malevolent spirits who plagued them. The alu was a hideous looking phantom that often appeared with one or more of its limbs missing and would attempt to envelope its victims in its clammy embrace. The most commonly seen ghost was the ekimmu, who would appear outside the house to give warning of an approaching death. These spirits often made dreadful wailing noises, and to hear these sounds was just as ominous as seeing the phantom. The Assyrians believed that all their ghosts resulted from either leaving a body unburied or else by failing to observe the due rites when a person died.

V

VALDEMAR

The grim phantom of Valdemar appears in Gurre Wood near Helsingor in Denmark whenever anything untoward is about to happen to the Danish royal family. The ghost is believed to be that of King Valdemar IV who, during his lifetime, was said to be gifted with the power of prophecy. Another Danish King, Abel, whom history credits with murdering his brother, is said to appear at Poole, near Slewig, also just prior to some crucial event in the affairs of the nation.

VALUATION GHOST

The case of the devaluation ghost occurred in Chicago in 1912 when a householder succeeded in getting the rateable value of his house reduced because it was haunted! The man, James Denlertander, of 3375 South Oakley Avenue, lodged a court appeal against the assessment of his premises on April 18, 1912, on the grounds that "a ghost has made it unprofitable for me." He told the tribunal that a girl had died in the house under mysterious circumstances and it was suspected she might have been murdered. Subsequently each new tenant had complained about hearing terrible moaning noises and cries of anguish and quit the premises within days. As a result of his appeal, the court reduced the valuation of Mr. Denlertander's house by *four thousand dollars!*

VAMPIRE GHOSTS

Vampire ghosts, as distinct from vampires, are recorded in the histories of several European countries, as well as India in particular. Such ghosts are usually invisible and occasionally attack human beings, leaving bite marks on the flesh. Throughout India there are whole classes of such spirits, known as Virikas, who have small, red-colored bodies, teeth like lions, and roam about at night making strange gibbering noises. In parts of the country small shrines are erected to leave offerings of food for the Virikas so that they do not go searching for human blood, and there is even a group of men known as the shaycana who have the power to drive away these vampire ghosts from any place they may be haunting. Europe also has a famous example of this kind of spirit in the case of the Romanian girl, Eleonore Zugun, who for several

Two small models of vampire ghosts made in Malaysia

years was constantly being bitten by a vampire ghost. It took a lengthy service of exorcism to drive off this vicious spirit, which covered her arms and neck with red teeth marks.

VARNEY THE VAMPIRE

Varney the Vampire is the title of one of the most famous "Penny Blood" serials written by a man named Thomas Peckett Prest (1810–59) and published in 1847. The serial was issued in penny weekly instalments and ran to 220 chapters and almost 1,000 pages before it was completed. For years the story was believed to be purely fictional, but recent research has shown that it may have been based on a case of ghostly vampirism that took place in the last years of the reign of Queen Anne of England. Apparently there were several reports at this time of a spirit that attacked its victims and left scratch marks on their bodies. *Varney the Vampire* was only the second novel to be written about the undead, *The Vampyre* by Dr. John Polidori, Lord Byron's secretary, being the first in 1816.

VAUCLUSE GAP GHOST

The famous 170-foot cliff known as the Gap at Vaucluse in Sydney, Australia, is said to have several ghosts, presumably of the unfortunate people who have jumped or fallen from the cliff. Extraordinary confirmation of one of these spirits emerged on September 22, 1959, when a New Zealand tourist discovered a ghostly figure in a photograph he took of the cliff. In the picture was the misty shape of a man just about to leap over the edge of the Gap.

VEAL, MRS., GHOST OF

The extraordinary tale of Mrs. Veal's ghost, which was published as an anonymous pamphlet under the title *The True Relation of the Apparition of One Mrs. Veal* in 1706 has a special place in ghost lore, for although it was believed to be a piece of fiction, subsequent enquiry established it was in fact a true case. This research also revealed that the author was none other than the great Daniel Defoe (1660–1731) later to write the classic *Robinson Crusoe* (1720). According to several authorities, the story of Mrs. Veal qualifies Defoe as "the founding father of supernatural fiction" and not surprisingly it still continues to be a staple selection for any anthology with pretensions at representing the development of the genre. Apart from several other short items related to the supernatural, Defoe also wrote *An Essay on the Reality of Apparitions* (1727).

Daniel Defoe, who is said to be the "founding father of supernatural fiction" through writing the story of Mrs. Veal's Ghost in 1706

VENGEFUL GHOSTS

The history of the supernatural contains numerous stories of ghosts returning to revenge themselves on those who wronged them, but the case of

The ghost of Christopher Slaughterford, who came looking for vengeance—and achieved it—in 1709

Christopher Slaughterford in the autumn of 1709 remains perhaps the most famous. Earlier that year, Slaughterford had been arrested in Guildford, England, and accused of murdering his wife-to-be, Jane Young. Although he protested his innocence and the evidence against him was scanty, Slaughterford was duly convicted and removed to the Marshalsea Prison in Southwark where he was hanged, still denying his guilt. Within days, his ghost was reported in Guildford, complete with the chains that had bound him during his trial, as well as in the prison wailing mournfully over his unjust execution. Later came his most dramatic appearance—to his former servant, Joseph Lee. This time the ghost of Slaughterford was carrying a flaming torch in one hand and had a rope around his neck. After a repeat of this appearance, the terrified Lee ran away in panic and was later found hanged—the evidence indicating that he was the man who had actually killed Jane Young.

VERRE GHOSTS

The Verre Tribe of Northern Nigeria have a special address that is read over the bodies of the dead just before they are buried in the hope of preventing them returning as ghosts. The exhortation reads: "You have lived long. Go now to the sun and declare that you are the last of living men and it is useless to send for any more of us. And do not bear us malice. Return not to earth to interfere with our crops or prevent our women bearing children." The history of this ghost tradition and others is discussed by Sir James Frazer in his important study *Fear of the Dead* (1933–6).

VERSAILLES GHOSTS

The story of two scholarly English lady tourists who apparently saw a whole group of ghosts in the gardens of the Trianon near Versailles in 1901 is now widely regarded as a classic encounter. The experience began on a hot August afternoon in 1901 as the two ladies, Miss C. A. E. Moberly and Miss E. F. Jourdain, were on their way to look at the Petit Trianon after walking around the lovely palace of Versailles. The ladies were interested in the Trianon, for they knew it to be a little retreat that Louis XVI had created for his queen, Marie Antoinette, as a place of relaxation for her and her courtiers. However, they had some difficulty finding the Trianon, and were soon conscious of a strangely chilling and rather depressing atmosphere around them. Then, all of a sudden, they came across a group of people dressed in costumes over a hundred years old. Puzzled, Miss Moberly and Miss Jourdain walked on, and were soon conscious of another change in the atmosphere back to the normal humidity of an August afternoon. For some time they debated over what they had seen—and reached the amazing yet seemingly undeniable fact that they had stepped back in time to the year 1789 and actually mingled with some ladies and gentlemen of the court of Marie Antoinette! So convinced were they of their extraordinary encounter that they published a report of it called *An Adventure* in 1911, and it has remained both a popular and puzzling book ever since. Several writers have subsequently investigated the story, including J. R. Sturge-Whiting, who maintains in his *The Mystery of Versailles* (1938) that the "sighting" can be explained logically, and Lucille Iremonger, whose *The Ghosts of Versailles* (1957) is a most thorough and fair-minded examination. Recently, in *Encounter* magazine (October 1976) a solution was put forward by Dr. Joan Evans that what the ladies really saw was a rehearsal of a tableau vivant being staged by the Comte Robert de Montesquiou-Fezenac. The ladies could not have known, says the report, that the Comte was in the habit of living out his eighteenth-century fantasies in this way. However, defenders of Miss Moberly and Miss Jourdain have been quick to point out that similar courtly figures have been seen since in the same location in 1908, 1928 and 1955 and none of these people had read *An Adventure*. So the mystery of Versailles continues.

VILLIERS'S GHOST

The remarkable sixteenth-century ghost story of Villiers's Ghost of England concerns a spirit that materialized in Windsor Castle and announced that it was the father of the Duke of Buckingham, George Villiers. The phantom warned that unless the Duke mended his ways and attempted to become more popular with his people, he would die very soon. When little notice was taken of the first warning, the spirit returned to underline his message. Apparently the ghostly warning still went unheeded, and true to the prophecy the Duke was assassinated by one of his unhappy followers.

A contemporary engraving of the ghost of George Villiers that brought an ominous prediction for the future

VINGOE FIRE

Vingoe Fire is a curious, ghostly phenomenon reported to occur before the death of a member of the Vingoe family who held the Treville estate near Cornwall, England. The family were said to be descended from Count de Treville, wine-taster to William the Conqueror, who accompanied his master to England and was rewarded with the Cornish estate. Ghost-hunter Elliott O'Donnell recounts the legend of Vingoe Fire, which occurred for several centuries, in his book *Family Ghosts and Ghostly Phenomena* (1933):

> Over the caves in the cliff on the estate is a carn, and on this, always prior to a death in the Vingoe family, flames would be seen, accompanied by strange and appalling noises. The phenomena would first appear as a full and glimmering light. Then, gradually, there would be spurts of flame, which would get larger and larger, and more and more lurid and ghastly. In the interval between the flashes, the surrounding objects, which had been rendered visible, would recede into a darkness that was sinister and terrible. Sometimes the flames would form a sort of chain or a series of chains, and sometimes they would make a large circle or ring; but their significance was invariably the same—the impending death of a Vingoe.

VIRGINIA, "THE GHOST STATE"

Virginia is said to be our most haunted state, while the town of Fredericksburg there is also widely held to be among the most ghost-ridden spots in the United States. The popular explanation for these facts is that a great many famous people lived there—George Washington, John Paul Jones, James Monroe and so on—and it is their shades that haunt the vicinity. However, the best-known of all the ghosts is the lady in white who haunts the beautiful old eighteenth-century Chatham Manor that overlooks Fredericksburg. This lady is said to be the spirit of a young woman who was frustrated in love and returns every seven years on the anniversary of her death, June 21. Fort Monroe, built in 1609 and the nation's longest manned army post, also boasts a splendid roll-call of phantoms, including those of General Robert E. Lee, General U. S. Grant, Abraham Lincoln, Jefferson Davis, the writer Edgar Allan Poe and the Indian Chief Black Hawk. According to eyewitnesses, Jefferson Davis, who was President of the Confederacy, appears most frequently. The only claim Virginia cannot match is to contain America's most haunted city. That honor belongs to New Orleans, which has over two dozen constantly reported phantoms; by far the majority of these in the atmospheric old French Quarter.

VIRIKAS

Virikas are the ghosts of India, small, hideous spirits who appear at night gibbering in a harsh, gutteral tone. They are red in color and have long, sharp

An illustration of one of the ghosts said to haunt the state of Virginia, taken from an old history of the town of Fredericksburg

teeth somewhat in the tradition of the vampire. Less unpleasant are two other types of Indian ghost, the paisachi and the bauta, who appear in the more traditional misty shapes of men and women and are believed to be omens of death. The Indians have always shown great respect for their ghosts and in many parts of the country have built small shrines to them where little gifts of flowers and food are left to keep them happy. If any Indian family is particularly troubled by a ghost they can always call upon the services of a shaycana, a venerable old man said to have the power to drive off troublesome spirits.

VISIONS OF CHILDREN

In her book *My Life as a Search for the Meaning of Mediumship* (1968), Mrs. Eileen Garrett has recounted details of a number of visions experienced by children in which they have described seeing the ghosts of deceased parents or grandparents. Despite the skepticism towards such accounts because of the youth of the viewers, Mrs. Garrett believes that many can be substantiated because of how positive the child is and the detailed nature of the description of the ghostly figure.

VOICES OF THE DEAD

There are numerous accounts of human beings hearing the voices of people they know have died, and some of the best examples are to be found in Camille Flammarion's work, *Death and Its Mysteries* published in 1864. In a well-authenticated, but slightly different case, one which occurred during the First World War, a mother in Indiana suddenly heard what she thought was her son, who was serving as a soldier in France, calling for help. She fell on her knees and prayed for him to be saved wherever he was. Two months later, in reply to a letter she had written to the boy, the mother learned that her son had indeed been shot and wounded at the very moment she had "heard" his cry. In a book entitled *Breakthrough—An Amazing Experiment in Electronic Communication with the Dead* (1971), a German psychologist, Dr. Konstantin Raudive, claimed to have recorded many thousands of ghost voices. Raudive (1909–74) became intrigued with the idea of trying to contact the spirits of the dead as a result of some extraordinary experiences while pursuing his hobby of recording bird songs. He therefore set up his recording equipment and, under the watchful eye of two observers, called on the dead to speak to him. A variety of responses was recorded, sometimes in different languages, sometimes audible, sometimes mere babbling, but the cumulative effect was extraordinarily positive, as Dr. Raudive describes in his intriguing book.

WAGGRAKINE PHANTOM

The phantom of Waggrakine, a small town seven miles from Geraldton in Australia, is a chilling ghost that has frightened a good many people over the years. The haunting is centered in an old cottage—believed to be well over a hundred years old—that had an evil reputation even before its third occupant, an elderly recluse, drowned himself in the adjacent well. Now on the anniversary of his death, the phantom of the old man is said to rise from the well, clad in the white nightshirt in which he died, and ringing a mournful bell.

WALPOLE, HORACE (1717–97)

Horace Walpole was the author of *The Castle of Otranto* (1764), the classic ghost novel that founded the Gothic horror story genre. Writing of the importance of this book, R. E. Budd says in *A Survey of the Occult* (ed., Julian Franklyn, 1935):

> Walpole's book is the earliest example of the Gothic romance by a generation, sets the fashion of housing its blatantly crude spectre in a gloomy Gothic castle liberally provided with secret passages, trap-doors and dungeons, and of seeking nightmare effects by the introduction of the tolling of bells, the flitting of owls and bats, horrid groans, unearthly music, and such accompaniments of ghostly visitation as uproar in the heavens, prodigious thunder-claps, an unnatural chill in the atmosphere and a tendency on the part of candles and lamps to burn with an eerie blue flame. Other disturbing phenomena are the armed apparition, of such vastness that even a spacious Gothic castle permits only of its appearance piecemeal; the portrait which utters deep sighs, heaves its breast, and quits its panel with a grave and melancholy air; the statue which discharges three drops of blood from its nose by way of protest against a proposed marriage and later dilates to enormous proportions in order to render more impressive its valedictory prophecy; and the praying friar who, on close examination, reveals "the fleshless jaws and empty sockets of a skeleton, wrapt in a hermit's cowl." By such devices did the Gothic romancers seek to terrorise their readers.

Walpole, who was the son of a British Prime Minister, wrote over thirty other books and achieved a kind of notoriety as a result of the house he transformed into a Gothic castle at Strawberry Hill, Twickenham. He also wrote a number of supernatural short stories that were finally collected in 1902 as *Unpublished Tales*, as well as one other weird novel entitled *The Mysterious Mother* (1768).

Horace Walpole's *The Castle of Otranto* (1764) was the novel that created the Gothic horror story genre

WALPURGIS NIGHT

The night of April 30 is known throughout Europe as *Walpurgisnacht* or Walpurgis Night, and it is the night when ghosts and the spirits of darkness are on the loose. Witches, in particular, are free to hold their ghastly revels as soon as the sun has set. The night gets its name from St. Walpurga, who is regarded as the protector of humanity against evil magic. She was actually the daughter of the Saxon King Richard and went with St. Boniface to Germany over twelve hundred years ago. There she so distinguished herself in the campaigns against demonism that she was made Abbess of Heidenheim. She was canonized about the year A.D. 777.

WASHINGTON, GEORGE (1732–99)

George Washington allegedly saw an apparition during the bleak winter of 1777 while he was camped with his troops in Valley Forge. The ghost took the form of a beautiful woman who appeared to Washington in his quarters and said in an ethereal voice, "Son of the Republic, look and learn!" She then gave him a vision of how America might become if he did not use his influence to see that peace was restored to the land and all men were allowed to live in equality. The truth or otherwise of this story has never been fully verified as it was not published until some sixty years after Washington's death.

WATER WRAITH

Water wraiths are peculiar to Scotland, according to J. M. McPherson in his *Primitive Beliefs in the North East of Scotland* (1929). They are skinny, withered old women with scowling features who dress all in green and apparently do their best to lure unwary travellers to their death by drowning. Mr. McPherson has made a point of the fact that in a number of the accounts of water wraiths the victims have been people returning home rather the worse for wear after a night's drinking!

WELLS, HERBERT GEORGE (1866–1946)

Though H. G. Wells is most famous as the "father of science fiction," he was also interested in the supernatural and wrote a number of short stories featuring ghosts including "The Red Room" and "The Story of the Inexperienced Ghost," which formed a delightfully amusing segment in the classic horror film *Dead of Night* made in 1946. According to a recent report, Wells has returned as a ghost to haunt his former Georgian terraced house in Hampstead, and a book has also been published that is claimed to be "spirit

An amusing moment from "The Story of the Inexperienced Ghost," one of several ghostly tales written by H. G. Wells

revelations" from the great author, *Bertie: The Life After Death of H. G. Wells* by Elizabeth Hawley and Columbia Rossi (1973).

WENDIGO

The wendigo is a Canadian entity, half phantom, half beast, who lives in the forests and preys on human beings, particularly children. The belief in this horror dates back to the earliest Indian legends and it is said that the wendigo will eat the flesh of its victims. According to R. S. Lambert in *Exploring the Supernatural* (1955), "Wendigos (who might be women as well as men) were believed to have entered into a pact with evil spirits, lurking in the forest, who helped them kill their victims." The legend of this creature has been immortalized in Algernon Blackwood's short story *The Wendigo* (1907). In W. T. Cox's *Fearsome Creatures of the Lumber Woods* (1951) a number of other Canadian "wood horrors" are listed, including the hodag, the whimpus, the hoop-snake, the celofay and the filamaloo.

WEREWOLF GHOST

The werewolf is, of course, a creature of folklore that can change from man into wolf and back again. But there are also a number of stories in Europe of werewolf ghosts, spirits that have returned from the dead as shape-changers. The most famous of these stories concerns England's heartless and cruel King John, who was said to have been poisoned and then risen again as a werewolf to terrorize the countryside. Two more recent examples come from the nineteenth century. In Cumberland the shadowy figure of a werewolf created widespread panic for some years until an arrangement of wolf and human bones was found in a cave and burned, thereby putting a stop to the terror. And at the end of the century in Wales a giant ghost wolf was regularly seen at large until a wolf skull was located, carefully exorcized, and then smashed into dust. The only current werewolf-ghost haunts the town of Flixton in Yorkshire, changing from man into beast, and glaring with blood-red eyes at anyone unfortunate enough to cross its path. Elliott O'Donnell devotes a chapter to werewolf ghosts in his *Casebook of Ghosts* (1969).

WEST POINT GHOST

The United States Military Academy at West Point is haunted by the ghost of a soldier in full Jackson era uniform who died almost 150 years ago. A number of cadets have reported seeing his impressive phantom complete with shako and musket. The haunting began on October 21, 1972, when a cadet in Room 4714 of 47th Division Barracks awoke to see the life-size apparition of a nineteenth-century officer emerge from a wall. The cadet immediately noticed how cold the room had suddenly become, but before he could shout and wake up his roommate, the ghost disappeared. The following night, however, both young men saw the phantom, and on other occasions several more cadets also saw the soldier, who was identified from a print in the West Point Gallery. The Military Academy is also said to be haunted by the ghost of an Irish cook who has been seen in the superintendent's mansion on several occasions.

WHITE HOUSE GHOST

Although there are stories of several ghosts being seen in the White House, the best authenticated phantom is that of Abraham Lincoln. Both residents and visitors claim to have seen Lincoln, including Theodore Roosevelt who said, "I think of Lincoln, shambling, homely, with his sad, strong deeply furrowed face all the time. I see him in the different rooms and halls." The ghost has apparently been seen by someone in every administration since Lincoln's assassination in 1865, a famous account being that of the First Lady Grace Coolidge, who said that the former President appeared to her "dressed in black, with a stole draped over his shoulders to ward off the draughts and chills." When Queen Wilhelmina of Holland stayed at the White House in the Rose Room, which is particularly associated with Lincoln, she is said to have heard a knock on the door and opened it to be confronted by the ghostly figure of the former President. In more recent times still, Sir Winston Churchill experienced an eerie sensation in the Rose Room, while Lady Bird Johnson felt a "chilling presence" while watching a TV special about Lincoln's death. It is perhaps not surprising that Lincoln's ghost should haunt the White House, for he was known to be psychic and his great interest in the supernatural caused him to allow a seance to be held in the Crimson Room in April 1863. Apparently for about half an hour various phenomena were seen, raps were heard and tables were moved about. Until the day of his death, President Lincoln remained convinced of the possibility of communication with the spirit world—and since then, according to psychic investigators, has been proving it by reappearing in his former home. The full story of the haunted White House is told in *Prominent American Ghosts* by Susy Smith (1967).

The best authenticated ghost in America may well be that of Abraham Lincoln, whose spirit is said to haunt the White House

WHITE LADIES

White ladies are a type of ghost found quite frequently in the British Isles in castles and very old houses, and are often the spirits of noblewomen who were murdered or died in tragic circumstances. They are also widely known in France, where they are said to be strikingly beautiful and most often found in the vicinity of bridges. The reason for this, according to an old French legend, is that it was once the custom to offer young women as human sacrifices to the rivers so that they would allow people to cross in safety. As in Britain, the white ladies of France have been reported in old castles and chateaux where they wander along the passageways, sometimes carrying cups of poison in their hands.

WHITE LADY OF THE HOHENZOLLERNS

The White Lady of the Hohenzollerns is another well-known German ghost and has been reported appearing at a number of former royal residences in Germany, including the castle of Neuhaus (where she has been most seen) and at Berlin, Bechin, Tretzen and Raumleau. These stories have naturally given rise to the suggestion that there is more than one ghost haunting the unfortunate Hohenzollern family! What the reports do agree upon is that the ghostly lady is dressed all in white and wears what looks like a widow's band on her head. George Doring has written a full account of the white lady in *The Iris* (1819), based on several eyewitness encounters. He shares the most widely held theory that the ghost is Princess Bertha, or Perchta von Rosenberg, who was cruelly treated by her husband, Baron Steyermark, and after her death in 1451 returned by way of retribution to haunt Neuhaus. It is also said that her appearances usually occurred just before the death of a member of the Prussian royal family.

WHOOPING HOLLOW

Few places in America are believed to be more haunted than Whooping Hollow in New England, according to Elliott O'Donnell in his book *Dangerous Ghosts* (1954). The locality is said to have earned its strange name as a result of an Indian battle fought there several centuries ago. A medicine-man from the defeated tribe cursed the area and vowed that his ghost would return to plague the hollow, uttering a terrifying whooping sound. Since then the sound of this cry has made Whooping Hollow a place to be avoided by all but the bravest souls.

WICKED LADY FERRERS

The building known as Markyate Cell near Dunstable in England is haunted by the ghost of Wicked Lady Ferrers, a beautiful and outrageous young woman who secretly became a highway robber in the seventeenth century in

White ladies are a familiar type of ghost throughout Europe, and are usually the spirits of women who have been murdered or ill-used

order to bring a little excitement into her otherwise drab life. Having made a secret passageway in and out of the house, Lady Ferrers would slip away under the cover of darkeness and, disguised as a man, rob and if necessary kill travellers on nearby Watling Street. However, after one confrontation she was badly wounded and only just had the strength to get back to Markyate Cell before she collapsed and died. When her body was discovered, still in the highwayman's outfit, her secret life was revealed. Not long afterwards, her ghost appeared and was seen either in the mansion, galloping along the local roads or, for a reason difficult to discern considering she was never brought to justice, hanging from a tree in the grounds! According to Christina Hole, who tells the story of Wicked Lady Ferrers in her book *Haunted England* (1940), she has continued to be seen well into this century.

WILD EDRIC

Whenever England is threatened with war, says an old Shropshire legend, Wild Edric and his followers ride out from the old lead mine where they dwell to do battle with the enemy. This ghostly troop always rides off in the direction from which the opposing forces are said to be coming, and were last reliably reported to have been seen by two people at Minsterley just before the start of the Crimean War. Edric, as head of the group, was dressed in green clothes and cloak with a white feather in his cap, while by his side rode a beautiful woman also in green with long blonde hair and known as Lady Godda. The legend maintains that Edric was actually a real person, the nephew of Edric Streona, Ealdorman of Mercia, and it was he who led the men of Shropshire when they rose against William the Conqueror. He was never defeated, but eventually made peace with William, and settled down with his wife, the Lady Godda, who some say was a fairy wife. The story of how Wild Edric rides out in troubled times is related in Christina Hole's *Haunted England* (1940).

WILD HUNT

The legend of the Wild Hunt is found all over northern Europe, and in its original form it was the god Woden on his white horse who led the hunt across the skies and brought death or disaster to all who watched him pass. The huntsmen are said to be the spirits of the restless dead and, as they fly overhead, the spectral dogs that often accompany them make strange howling sounds that invariably set off the earthly dogs below. According to Christina Hole in *Haunted England* (1940), the wild huntsman can always be recognized by his broad-brimmed hat and his wide mantle, from which he is surnamed Hakelbarend, an old word signifying mantle-wearer. An owl named Tutursel and a flight of ravens also accompany the hunt. Quoting an old authority, Miss Hole says:

> Whoever sees it approach must fall flat on the ground, or shelter himself under an odd number of boards, nine or eleven, otherwise he will be borne away through the air and set down hundreds of miles from his home. . . . It is

The fearsome Wild Hunt, which is widely believed to be an omen of disaster

> still more dangerous to look out of the window when Woden is sweeping by. The rash man is struck dead, or at least he gets a box on the ear that makes his head swell as big as a bucket and leaves a fiery mark on his cheek. In some instances the offender is struck blind or mad. There are certain places where Woden is accustomed to feed his horse or let it graze, and in those places the wind is always blowing.

Miss Hole adds that in more recent times the wild huntsmen have been "superseded by the spectral coach."

WILD WEST GHOSTS

The legendary blood-soaked Wild West is, not surprisingly, believed to be haunted by many ghosts, both those of Indians who died trying to prevent the encroachment of the white men onto their lands and those of the later gunfighters and lawmen who used guns and rifles to settle their disputes. A famous Indian ghost is that of a huge spectral warrior who rides the range in Wyoming and is believed to be the spirit of a tribal chief who was tricked into selling his people's land to cattlemen and must now do penance by endlessly riding his old hunting grounds. In Colorado, the ghost of Chief Little Owl wanders the land he and his tribe hunted before the advent of the white men. There are numerous phantoms reported on the sites of Indian massacres, such as Mount Diablo in California, and the blood-drenched Sand Creek in Colorado where 200 Indians were slaughtered in 1864. Eerie, wailing spirits are also said to wander about the famous site of Wounded Knee in South Dakota, where over 200 Sioux Indians were butchered by soldiers in 1890. The ghosts of white men, women and children also haunt the pioneer trails where they were massacred by the Indians—trials like the Oregon Trail, the Santa Fe Trail and the California trail. Death Valley in California got its name from a party of thirteen men who died there in 1849 and their ghosts are still occasionally seen. The gold rush, which made some men's fortunes and took the lives of many others, left numbers of phantoms behind to wander unhappily around the appropriately named "ghost towns." Among the ghosts of famous outlaws that still ride the West should be mentioned Jesse James, who appears in a number of places where he carried out his robberies, including the town of Lawrence in Kansas; and Billy the Kid, who has been sighted in Fort Sumner, New Mexico, where he was killed. Of the lawmakers, Wyatt Earp haunts Tombstone, Arizona where he had his famous shootout, and the great Indian fighter Wild Bill Hickok has been seen in Deadwood, South Dakota, still wearing the buckskin outfit that made him so instantly recognizable when he was alive.

WILL-O'-THE-WISP

Will-o'-the-wisp is probably the most popular name in Europe for the mysterious, ghostly lights that are seen hovering or moving about near graveyards or over marshy areas. Among their other names are jack-o'-lantern, fairy fire, corpse light, corpse candle, William with the little flame, and many more. One old tradition says they are the souls of dead people, appearing either as an omen of death or else guarding lost treasure; while another belief claims they are wandering souls that cannot enter either heaven or hell, and have therefore become malignant and do their best to lead those foolish enough to follow them into danger. Recent research into the will-o'-the-wisp has suggested that it is actually caused by the igniting of gases escaping from rotting animal or plant matter.

WOLHAARHOND

The wolhaarhond is the South African phantom dog—a large, woolly creature that glows in the darkness. From a distance the dog appears like a red light and its actual shape only materializes when it gets close to anyone unfortunate enough to cross its path. Eric Rosenthal discusses this creature and several other animal phantoms in his book *They Walk By Night* (1949).

WOLSEY'S GHOST

The strange story of the ghost of one leading member of the English Church appearing to another was the subject of a best-selling pamphlet published in 1641. The title of this now extremely rare publication complete with its quaint woodcut of the meeting tells the whole story, "Canterbury's Dream: In Which The Apparition of Cardinal Wolsey did Present Himself unto Him on the Fourteenth of May Last Past." The anonymous author of the work (probably a churchman) is reluctant to impart details of the conversation between man and ghost, except that Wolsey warned of dire times ahead for the people of England unless they turned again to God. It was, of course, a

The ghost of Cardinal Wolsey appearing to another high churchman, the Archibishop of Canterbury, in 1641; from a contemporary pamphlet

prophetic warning—for the following year the English Civil War between Charles I and Oliver Cromwell began.

WOODSTOCK GHOST

The account of the uproarious haunting of Woodstock Palace during the English Civil War is one of the lighter moments in the history of the supernatural. The Parliamentarians were, of course, strict Puritans and inclined to take anything untoward as the work of the Devil himself, so that the party of Cromwell's men who went to Woodstock, a former Royal residence, to remove all traces of the King's occupancy, were ill-prepared for what occurred there in 1649. Within days of their arrival-appropriately on Friday, October 13—the Cromwellians found their sleep being disturbed by strange noises, weird figures were seen drifting along the passageways, and all manner of household articles began mysteriously flying through the air. Panic quickly set in among the party and when one man nearly killed another coming across him in a darkened passageway wearing only a long, white nightshirt and looking for all the world like a ghost, they abandoned their mission and fled. The story naturally enough soon spread that the palace was haunted, and it was therefore given a wide berth by the Parliamentarians for the rest of the Civil War. However, as soon as the Restoration of the monarchy took place, a former clerk at Woodstock, Joseph Collins—known locally as a practical joker and nicknamed "Funny Joe"—confessed that he had been responsible for the haunting, devising all the ghostly manifestations to frighten the intruders away! The famous illustration here illustrates what has since become a classic case of a phony haunting.

The riotous "haunting" at Woodstock in which a group of Cromwell's men were terrified by a practical joker in 1649

WORTH, PATIENCE

Patience Worth was a seventeeth-century English girl who went to America and was there killed by Indians. Three centuries later in 1916 she became the subject of an amazing controversy. In that year a medium named Mrs. John Curran of St. Louis claimed to have made contact with Patience, who proceeded to dictate a host of literary works all in authentic seventeeth-century language. Mrs. Curran's claim was extensively investigated and the facts about Patience Worth were, one by one, proved to be true. Dr. Walter Prince, who was one of the investigators, later wrote a book, *The Riddle of Patience Worth* (1926), which added weight to the claim that the story was "one of the outstanding phenomenons of the age."

WOTAN

For generations throughout Europe, a storm was thought to herald the arrival of Wotan, "the Wild Huntsman," a phantom who rode the skies with his spectral hounds in search of human souls to capture. In parts of France, rural people still lock their doors when a wild wind gets up, half believing that the evil horseman might spot them and carry them off, as tradition says he did to their forebears in the past.

WRAITHS

The wraith is a ghost of a person on the verge of death. According to the old traditions, it appears as an exact likeness of its human counterpart, showing itself to relatives or friends of that person as he is about to die. Naturally they are regarded as a death omen, and should a person see a wraith of himself then his days are also numbered. The most famous instance of this happening occurred to the poet Percy Shelley (1792–1822), who saw his own wraith just as he was stepping on board a small boat that was to take him across the Bay of Spezia in Italy to the town of Leghorn and a reunion with his friend, Leigh Hunt. The boat foundered in a storm, of course, and Shelley was drowned, thus fulfilling the tradition of the wraith. According to Reverend Frederick Lee in his *Examples of the Supernatural* (1894), the tradition of the wraith appears to have developed from a very old belief that a person's soul is an exact duplicate of his or her living body, and that it must escape from the body when death is imminent. A variation of this ghost is the water wraith, a spirit that haunts stretches of water, one of the most famous examples of which appears on the River Conon near Brahan Castle in Scotland. Whenever the spirit has been seen, say local reports, a drowning has occurred not long afterwards.

A wraith as described in Reverend Frederick Lee's *Examples of the Supernatural* published in 1894

WU

The wu are Chinese mediums who allow themselves to be possessed by the spirits of dead people and thereby communicate messages to the living. These specially gifted people are said to be most effective in reaching the departed if a feast is held in honor of the dead person and he or she is then invited to attend the celebrations. Apparently Chinese ghosts are somewhat class-conscious, for records indicate they usually only attend when summoned by members of the professional or Mandarin classes!

XENOGLOSSIE

Xenoglossie was the term coined by Professor Charles Richet to describe spirit mediums speaking or writing in unknown languages. From the early years of spiritualism in America, it became common for certain trance mediums to pass on messages in foreign languages of which they claimed to have no knowledge, or else in tongues that no one had ever heard before. Professor Richet discusses this and other aspects of his work in *Thirty Years of Psychical Research* (1923).

YARRALUMIA HOUSE GHOST

The picturesque and imposing Yarralumia House in Canberra, Australia is said to be haunted by a small, dark ghost that skulks in the undergrowth. The house is the residence of the Governor-General and stories of the phantom have been reported by several generations of servants. According to one account, the spirit is that of an Aboriginal servant who is searching for a very valuable diamond believed to be hidden under one of the garden's many deodar trees.

YEATS'S GHOST

The story of the haunting of Renvyle House in Connemara, County Galway, and the ghost that the famous Irish poet W. B. Yeats (1865–1939) is said to have raised there, is one of the most fascinating tales to be found in Ireland. According to one account, Yeats reached the spirit through automatic writing and learned that it objected to people occupying its former room. The

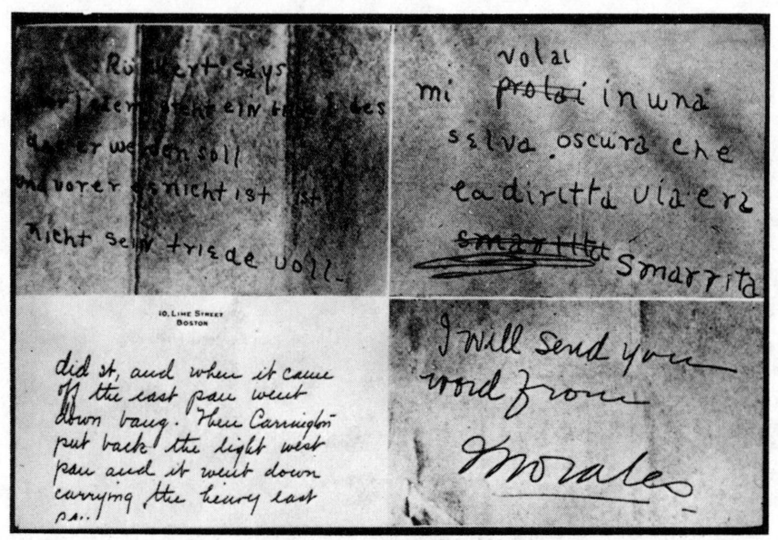

An example of xenoglossie—spirit messages produced in a variety of handwritings and languages

poet then extracted a promise from the ghost that if the room was closed to visitors it would cease haunting. All did indeed remain quiet until a particularly curious guest defied the order—and at this the ghost returned once more. The house is now a hotel, but previously belonged to another Irish man of letters, Oliver St. John Gogarty, and it was he, knowing full well of the place's reputation for being haunted, who arranged a number of seances in the late 1920s—which Yeats attended—in an attempt to contact the ghost. According to Peter Underwood in his account of the haunting in his book, *Gazetteer of Scottish and Irish Ghosts* (1973), "Yeats is credited with personally raising the ghost of a previous occupant of the house, a man who is said to have strangled himself with his bare hands and whose restless ghost still walks here. More than one visitor has insisted on changing rooms, but few ever offer any explanation for wanting to move." Mr. Underwood adds that many people now believe Renvyle House to be the most haunted house in Ireland and there is even a suggestion that another tall, ethereal figure has joined in the haunting—this being the ghost of W. B. Yeats himself!

YELLOW MAN

According to a persistent legend, the fate of the French nation is somehow connected with the appearance of a ghost known as the "Yellow Man." This strange phantom with a yellow face and a red mark around his throat is first reported to have been seen in 1870 shortly before the outbreak of the Franco-German War. Writing about the ghost in *Family Ghosts and Ghostly Phenomena* (1933), Eliott O'Donnell says,

> Those who survived the war and remembered seeing the "Yellow Man," as they termed the apparition, were of the opinion that it was inexplicably

Eleanore Zugun, the young Romanian girl who was persistently attacked and bitten by an invisible spirit she called *Dracu*, or the Devil

connected with the fate of France, and that its manifestation had heralded the struggle in which France had been about to become engaged. The Yellow Man was seen again in the Chamber of Deputies by several people before the death of Gambetta, and also, collectively, in the same spot, the night before the assassination of President Carnot, and yet again in the same building in 1910. There is a rumor that its last appearance was a few days prior to the beginning of the Great War.

ZUGUN, ELEANORE (b. 1913)

Eleanore Zugun was a thirteen-year-old Romanian peasant girl who, in 1926, became world famous when she claimed to be the victim of vicious attacks by a phantom spirit she called *Dracu* (the Devil). She revealed scratch and bite marks on her hands and face that she said the ghost inflicted on her, and such was the bewilderment surrounding her story that she was taken to London to undergo extensive tests in the national Laboratory of Psychical Research. Under strictly controlled laboratory conditions, scratch marks were observed appearing on her body as well as teeth marks on her arms, and the leading investigator, Harry Price, declared himself convinced of the genuineness of the case. He was, however unable to decide precisely what caused the attacks, and the mystery has remained to this day. Mr. Price himself recounts the extraordinary case in his *Poltergeist Over England* (1945).

ZULULAND GHOST

An old battlefield at Iteleni in Zululand (part of Natal in South Africa) is said to be haunted by the ghost of Louis Napoleon, heir to the throne of France, who died in a battle there in 1879. The presence of the ghost first came to light on May 25, 1880, when the heartbroken Empress Eugénie made a pilgrimage to the spot where her only son had fallen. According to Eric Rosenthal in his book *They Walk By Night* (1949), the Empress found herself being guided by some supernatural agency to the meeting of two rough tracks. There something quite quite extraordinary happened to her, as she later reported: "Suddenly my nostrils were filled with the faint scent of verbena, the favourite perfume of my son, and I heard his voice murmuring, 'Mother, it was here.'" Since that date the actual figure of Louis Napoleon, dressed in battle uniform, has been several times reported in the same area.

Index

D

E

F

G

H

N

O

P

R

S

T

U

V

W

Y

Z